THE SELF-ESTEEM BOOSTER:

ROADMAP TO IMPROVE SELF CONFIDENCE, DEVELOP SELF LOVE AND ATTRACT THE RELATIONSHIPS YOU DESERVE.

ESTRELLA BERNHARD

Contents

Introduction 1

Believe In Yourself & Your Abilities 3

Carry Yourself With The Confidence Of A King 7

Qualities of People with High Self-Esteem 10

How Low Self-Esteem Impacts Your Life 11

Tips to Increase Your Confidence 15

Before you Speak 15

2. During Your Speech 19

3. After Your Speech 21

Additional Tips 22

Positive Reinforcement 27

Why Positive Reinforcement Works 28

How Positive Reinforcement Impacts Your Brain 29

How to Set Goals 30

How to Become Your Own Biggest Cheerleader 33

Healthy Body, Healthy Mind 35

How Physical Health Impacts Self-Worth 36

Stay Fit and Healthy 41

Social Networks 45

The Benefits of Social Media 46

Social Media and Self-Esteem 47

Unhealthy Social Media Practices 49

Healthy Social Media Practices 50

Connect with Yourself 53

Cultivate Your Skills 54

Accept Compliments 56

Practice Self-Compassion 57

Quick Boosts to Self-Esteem **61**
Power Poses 62
Dress With Confidence **69**
Fabulous & Easy Ways To Boost Your Self-Confidence 71
Building Self-esteem **79**
Using Affirmations to Change Your Thinking 86
Meditation For Confidence **89**
Feed Your Confidence **93**
Exercise for Confidence **95**
Confidence Builders That You Can Include In Your Daily Life ... **99**
Women & Confidence **103**
Develop Faith **105**
The ways in which you can involve yourself in Self-love **111**
Overcoming Struggles **129**
Laws Of Self-Love **133**
The Importance of Achieving Your Dreams **137**
Facts About Confident People **143**
Conclusion **145**

Introduction

Confidence is something that every person should carry within themselves. How we dress, act, walk, talk and interact with people all carries a huge weight when we speak of confidence. Confidence is what allows us to take risks and to really put ourselves out there without the fear of what others may think.

If you perform any task with confidence, you will greatly improve the results and you will really enjoy the process as well. You will find that as your confidence grows, your abilities will multiply or will appear to. Tasks that were so daunting in the past, will seem so easily completed now and you will begin to wonder why you never took the plunge sooner.

Confidence is something that should really be classified a superhuman strength because what you can achieve with this little ingredient is truly remarkable. You will suddenly find that people actually stop and listen and pay attention to what you are saying and that your opinions which were once, if ever spoken out, glanced over, are now center stage and of great value.

Confidence is a state of mind and cannot be learned or taught. It is the feeling of calm, quiet, sureness and belief that you can do whatever you set your mind to. You are the master of your own confidence and you alone can determine whether or not what others think will be allowed to influence you in any way.

Often people lack confidence because they have a low body image and are uncomfortable with how they look. This is easily overcome by learning about and exploring your own body. Be honest with yourself about your physical appearance and the strengths and shortcomings that go with it. Learn to highlight your strong features and draw attention away from the shortcomings. If you feel more comfortable with how you look, you will begin to feel more confident just being you and your confidence will get the much needed boost it needs.

Perhaps you feel you are not well-read or educated enough to offer your opinions and ideas. This feeling will definitely dent your confidence and comfort levels in a group situation. Take the opportunity to read as much as you can on whatever topic you can or even take that study course you have always wanted to but never got to. Increase your knowledge and you will begin to feel more confident sharing your opinions and ideas.

Many people who have made progress with their confidence levels suddenly go back a few steps when they happen to fail at something. This is by no means a reason to wilt away but rather an opportunity to take control and show your strength by persevering until you succeed. This will really show your worth and you will be respected for not giving up at the presentation of the smallest obstacle.

Nothing in life worth possessing is easy to obtain and if truth be told, nobody ever told you it was. Work hard for what you want, reach for your goals with hand outstretched and stride with confidence to the finish line.

“I am the master of my fate and the captain of my destiny” - Nelson Mandela

Believe In Yourself & Your Abilities

In life, we all have our demons to face and conquer. The hardest part is making that decision to put an end to it's reign over your life. Belief in yourself and your abilities is half the battle won already and if you continue on that path, steadfast in your own ambition and belief, you will succeed and the feeling when you do will be immeasurable.

A lack of confidence is often the result of having little or no belief in your own abilities and your own worth. Often these feelings come from external sources who break you down at every opportunity they get. The more negative feedback that surrounds your activities or opinions, the less confident you will feel speaking out for fear of being belittled once again.

Realize immediately that these very people who wish to break you down and belittle you, are the ones that fear your power when you are at your most confident. They realize exactly what you are capable of or will be capable of if allowed to freely show belief in yourself. These bullies, if we may call them that, have their own feelings of inadequacy which they are projecting onto you. They pass on these negative vibes in hopes that you will not outshine them. These are their own demons to face and conquer.

The sooner you decide to let go of any negativity and to stop worrying about what others will say or do, the happier and more confident you will become. As difficult as it may seem, make a concerted effort to simply wipe the thought of others from the slate and worry only about what you want to achieve and how that makes you feel. You will find that you begin to speak out more often on subjects that you have knowledge on and you will begin to show less fear in offering your own opinions and standing behind them. Tasks will come more easily and you will be more readily willing to take them on, secure in the knowledge that if you do fail, it doesn't matter what others say, you simply keep at it until you succeed. Your confidence will grow and your fears will decrease with every passing minute and with every completed task you will realize what great potential you actually have.

Confidence is not something that can be taught but is rather an awakening within you and a realization that you are worth more than what you think and your opinions and contributions are invaluable in any situation. For someone who feels inadequate and has no confidence in themselves, it can be a difficult prison to break free from but one from which the shackles must be broken if you are to go on and develop into the person you were created to be.

This is not something that will suddenly change overnight but is rather a lifelong work in progress. There are small little things that you can do each day to put you in the right frame of mind and ready to take on the day ahead.

- Lie quietly in the morning before you rise and surround yourself with positive thoughts, remind yourself of how talented and special you are and that you have so much to offer the world.

- Make a list of things you would like to accomplish and go for it, as your confidence grows with the small things, the large things will follow with ease.
- Be mindful to express appreciation for those who offer their opinions or complete tasks as they too may be someone who needs a boost in their own confidence and belief in their own abilities. You will find that this behavior is infectious and those around you will begin to do the same and perhaps your very oppressor will be the one to lighten the way for you.
- Recognize and be thankful for your strong points even though they may not be completely evident to all just yet, you know where your own strengths lie and you have only been waiting for the moment to let the world in on your secret.
- Forgive those who still try to overpower you and overshadow your brilliance. They don't yet realize that the problem they have with you is not really your problem to worry about but rather their problem to deal with.
- Try something new each day. Taking a risk or making a change is frightening but invigorating at the same time. All you have to do is believe in your own abilities.
- At the end of each day, before you lay your head down to rest, reflect on your day and make a vow to try again tomorrow if you failed at something or to perfect something that you have finally managed to complete. Recognize and accept your strengths and allow your confidence in your abilities to skyrocket.

As your confidence grows, be mindful not to gloat or become arrogant towards those who are still finding their feet. You know exactly where they are at the moment and how inadequate they are feeling and you of all people should realize the value of careful encouragement and spurring them on to succeed.

Yes, you shouldn't worry about what others think but it is human nature to pay attention to these details. Your brain has to be trained to think in a different pattern and to be honest, the mind and brain can be stubborn as a mule. This is why you need to constantly remind yourself of your goals and your worth and your complete ability, your mind may try to tell you otherwise and those around you may continue to try to break you down but you will find the strength to stand up and hold your ground as the confidence begins to shine from every pore of your being.

There will be moments where you experience weakness and these should never stop you from picking up and starting over. These moments are mere obstacles on your road to confidence and happiness. Giving up will be less enticing when you realize what you can actually achieve and when you begin to have belief in yourself and your abilities. You may encounter someone who is arrogant and will try with all his might to overpower you but don't play his games, his games is to feed his own demons. Stand strong and believe in yourself, have the courage to weather the storm and his harsh words will simply was away in the rain.

Carry Yourself With The Confidence Of A King

Your posture and the way you approach people can either portray you as confident and a force to be dealt with or it can portray you as feeble, insignificant and without your own opinions. If you carry yourself with the outward appearance of having confidence, you will begin to feel it inwardly a well.

Walk straight up, with your shoulders pushed backwards and your head held high and let those who you are approaching know that you mean business and that you won't go down without a fight. Hunching over makes you appear weak and feeble and even shy and this is not want you want.

Take meaningful strides when you walk, shuffling along will make you appear shy or even ill. Stepping with purpose lets people know you have somewhere you are going and you are not stopping until you reach that destination.

Eye contact is extremely important and allows the person you are speaking with to realize that you have conviction for what you are saying and that you want to engage with them on the topic. Speak directly and with a purpose. Shrinking back into your shell and avoiding their eyes will lead them to believe that they are stronger and that your opinions will not stand up against theirs.

Make sure that you attend your meeting prepared and that there is no chance that your feathers will be ruffled and send you back to that squirming, uncomfortable being that you fought so hard to free. You have gained that confidence that you so deserve and you really must do everything possible to retain your composure. As time passes, you will more easily be able to take on encounters that are unexpected and still maintain your confident edge. As with everything in life, confidence is a daily battle that must be fought continuously and is always a work in progress.

Pay careful attention to your body language and stop yourself from reverting back to any of your old traits, the traits that belong to the person you once were. It is very easy to slip back into habits without a thought and in some cases it may just be done subconsciously. Things like nail biting or fidgeting, signs that you doubt yourself which the new you does not. By no means should you appear rigid or stiff and as if you are trying not to fidget but a quiet stillness is the perfect opportunity to show you authority and your confidence.

When seated, use the entire space and look comfortable. Sitting on the edge of the seat or crunching up in a corner are not signs of your confidence but rather a lack of. If you sit comfortably and fill your space, your presence will be known.

Hiding your hands out of sight out of nervousness can portray dishonesty so keep those hands visible, loosely on your lap or even on your hips will do.

It is often easier to get your message across when you use hand gestures along with your verbal presentation. Keep the gestures open and it will give your hands something to do besides fidget.

Important points should be accompanies by the steepling of your hands in front of you on the table. Using this gesture shows authority and a great deal of confidence.

Keep your feet firmly on the ground. The tendency is to cross your legs but this projects a negative vibe, as does crossing your arms. Besides the negative vibe, it also portrays a lack of interest in what is being discussed. When standing, use a wide stancc and allow yourself to exude stability.

An easy, unforced smile is a wonderful way of opening the doors to discussion. A smile is friendly and invites the other party into the discussion with ease. A smile also shows that you are confident in your approach.

Beforc any planned encounter, prepare yourself, body and mind. Perhaps some light meditation and a little exercise to relieve tension and help you to keep calm and relaxed. If you feel calm, confident and relaxed, your body language will show it.

Your body reacts without your knowledge, like a knee jerk reaction. Become more aware of mood and feelings and make a concerted effort to take control of your own reactions and body. Do whatever it takes to calm you and instill you with confidence before a planned meeting and your body will play along and exude the quiet stillness and confidence you want the other party to recognize.

Self-esteem is an essential quality for anyone to have, but for many of us, it doesn't come naturally. Having a strong sense of self-esteem means that you are confident about your worth and abilities. Individuals who have a strong self-esteem tend to have a high level of self-respect and are capable of taking care of themselves in a way that allows them to be the best that they can be. More often than not, people with a strong sense of self-esteem are very helpful and caring, but they know how to be so without dismissing their own needs. The next sections discuss in depth what self-esteem is, what affects it, and how it can impact your life.

QUALITIES OF PEOPLE WITH HIGH SELF-ESTEEM

People who live with a healthy sense of self-esteem live with an attitude of humility. They feel confident when they do the things they know they are good at, and they are more than willing to do these in front of others without fear of judgment. Their positive self-esteem is further increased and affirmed when others recognize that they are good at what they do and praise them for a job well done.

Having a strong sense of self-esteem, they do not fear being criticized or rejected for having an opinion. For that reason, they find it easy and even essential to speak up about their truths, the things they believe in, and to assert themselves when they need to. Because they are confident in themselves, people with healthy self-esteem find it easy to speak about their convictions in a way that makes others more likely to receive it; at the same time, they do so without requiring the approval of others. In other words, while approval might be appreciated, it is not necessary.

Another great ability that people with self-esteem possess is knowing how to separate their feelings from the messages they are delivering. People who have strong levels of self-appreciation know how to separate emotions from the content of someone else's communication, making it easy for them to hear and appreciate the value of other people's opinions. Furthermore, they are capable of recognizing various emotions and the role they play in other people's lives. This means that they do not feel personally responsible for or victimized by how another person feels. They also try to look beneath the surface and see what is going on underneath so that they can be more mindful and kind toward others.

When an individual has a healthy sense of self-esteem, they also find it easier to release others and give them the freedom and space to make their own decisions. Because they are self-sufficient and capable of believing in and affirming themselves without the need for external approval, individuals with healthy self-esteem are able to honor and promote the same in others. They are great at allowing others to come to their own conclusions and learn from their own lessons; they do not feel the need to interject, intervene, or control other people's lives.

Another great effect of having a healthy self-esteem is that people will hold themselves accountable for their words and deeds. They always do what they say they will do because they know themselves—they recognize what they can do, within reason, and what they simply cannot. They are also great at leaving the past in the past and at appreciating the present for what it is, enabling them to act accordingly. Because people with a strong sense of self-esteem are capable of understanding that others are often emotionally driven, they can forgive and move forward, keeping themselves out of the painful "victim" position that holding grudges can put people into.

How Low Self-Esteem Impacts Your Life

Self-esteem has a major impact on how we live our lives. When people have a low sense of self-esteem, they are less likely to engage in things they love because they are fearful of what others will think. They may refrain from speaking passionately on topics they like, from honoring their truth, or from standing up for themselves when it is needed. Instead, they may become passive and allow others to bully them or push them around—or they may simply fade into the background because they are afraid of what other people's attention might bring.

Because it has the capacity to keep you from doing many things, having a low self-esteem can reduce the quality of the life you're living. You may find yourself avoiding places, things, and people that you love because you are afraid of what might happen. You fear that you will not be able to stand up or account for yourself. You may also begin to experience depression and anxiety, sometimes with tragic results, because you do not know how to handle or manage things as a result of your low self-esteem.

When you are caught in a place of low self-esteem, you may also find yourself holding onto grudges. This means that you stay in victim-mode for an extended period of time, blaming others for why you feel the way you do and struggling to forgive and move forward. You may even feel like the past is continually haunting you and you cannot seem to escape from it. These are all common side effects of having a low sense of self-esteem.

WHAT AFFECTS SELF-ESTEEM?

Through the course of our lives, our self-esteem can be affected by many things. Some people may experience low self-esteem as a result of their childhood, or it may develop later in adulthood as a result of abuse, excessive ongoing stress, or traumatic events. On the other hand, people may experience positive or healthy self-esteem because they have been adequately supported and encouraged throughout childhood and have gone on to experience equally healthy interactions in adulthood.

The common factors known to create low self-esteem are linked to early childhood. Those who were raised in abusive or dysfunctional homes in their formative years can have symptoms that reflect a negative impact on their self-esteem. They may find themselves feeling incapable of living up to someone's standards or regularly trying to fade into the background to avoid dysfunction and abuse. Generally, their idea of what normal interactions look like mirrors unhealthy ones, giving them a false perception of the world around them.

If low self-esteem is developed later in adulthood and was not present in childhood, it may be as a result of ongoing stress or traumatic events. For example, relationship breakdowns, struggles with family or career, incidents of bullying by coworkers or friends, financial burdens, and other such experiences common in adulthood can all contribute to reduced self-esteem. While these individuals will likely have an easier time regaining a healthy self-esteem due to having understood what possessing it felt like, it will still take time and practice to return to that point.

Individuals who have a healthy self-esteem in adulthood are believed to have been raised in a home that supports and encourages individuals, promoting their independence while also providing adequate support to achieve it. They are generally given many coping tools during their upbringing that allow them to feel confident about tackling life's adversities. As a result, these individuals will go on to experience happier and healthier adult lives.

Tips to Increase Your Confidence

Although there are many different ways to increase your confidence, and that it does not apply to everyone, we have selected some of the most common and effective practices to help you gain your confidence. Though the situations vary (so does your confidence), we can categorize everything into 4 main sections. We will cover the time before, during and after your speech/decision and the other situations not covered in the previous 3 common situations. We group them this way because, most of the time, you are not really aware of your confidence and it just drops when you need to speak up or when you are presented with a decision or opportunity. The tips we present in this book should cover all situations you will find yourself in.

Before you Speak

This covers the situation when you are asked to do something, or when you want to do something. For example, you are invited to a job interview. Otherwise, you want to ask somebody out for a date. What do you do? Remember: Groundwork is everything. You should gather your courage and find confidence in yourself from now. If you do not do it now, then it is hard to do so when you are up there doing a presentation or being interviewed or asking that lady out. Here are a few tips:

Know Yourself

Before you could tell yourself that you can do it and that you believe in your ability, you should know the limits of your ability first. Here, you should know what you are confident at and what you need to work on. Why do you need to do this?

If you know what you are good at, then you should act on your strength than your weaknesses. After all, if you are strong in a particular field, you should base your actions on that to ensure the highest degree of success. For example, if you know that you make really good jokes and that you want to ask a lady out, try to make her laugh and then ask her out. She will most likely say yes because she sees you are as a fun person. Plus, when you use your strengths to your advantage, your confidence will rise up as well.

Moreover, if you know what you need to work on, it makes everything a lot easier since you know exactly where you are lacking. You can then start planning to improve yourself accordingly. To illustrate, if you find yourself having a hard time doing public speaking, then you know that you should take a public speaking class or practice more at home or with your peers. That way, when you actually need to deliver that speech, you will see yourself improve while you are doing it. Then, with it comes that confidence.

Be Prepared

This goes hand-in-hand with knowing yourself. Arthur Ashe once said that confidence is a key to success, and the key to self-confidence is preparation. You just read an example about doing a public speaking. You cannot give a good speech without prior practice or preparation. In fact, preparation is a simple, yet effective method to boost your confidence. Suppose you need to speak on behalf of your company in an attempt to get people to invest in the company. The thing is, you need to speak for more than an hour in front of important people such as CEOs, directors, etc. Anyone would get nervous at this point. Why is that?

Most of the time, we do not feel confident because of our own ability, but rather because of the consequence. "What if I fail?" Sounds familiar? When you need to do a lot of things and have only one shot at it, and that the stakes are high, anyone would be at least a bit nervous. So, how do you improve your confidence in such a situation? Preparation. Lots of preparation.

Using the above example, you should study your company thoroughly. Know what it can deliver and try to come up with ways to convince them to invest in the company. It requires a lot of work, but when you have done everything, you know that all the information you need is at the back of your head. When we need to do a presentation, most people are not confident because they don't know what to speak, or even where to start. By familiarizing yourself with what you will be presenting, and arranging the presentation to your liking, you know that you can deliver a good presentation. Plus, with additional practice at home, you simply cannot fail.

Be Positive

Suppose that you are facing an overwhelming situation. Almost everything is stacked against you. You know that the road ahead will be difficult. What do you do? Stay positive. You don't quit. Never accept failure. Why is such a powerful mindset important?

There is a saying that there is always a sunshine after the storm. When you do not accept failure and remain hopeful and positive, you will eventually overcome that challenge and be more confident. In fact, failure only really comes when you give up. You never really fail if you don't.

To illustrate, if you are trying to learn how to code a program, but continue to fail time and again, it is natural to become frustrated and want to give up. Do not give up. Most of the time, all you really need is more time to learn and familiarize yourself with the process. Once you get it down, you can understand where you went wrong and fix it. Eventually, you will begin to see results and succeed. Once you do, you will feel that rush of excitement. That is a confidence booster. When another familiar program comes along, you know that you're willing to give it a shot. It is worth noting that growth, especially confidence, does not come with comfort. You need to do something that you don't think you can in order to improve that confidence.

The same could be said when you are presented with an opportunity. Suppose that you want to apply for a scholarship to a famous university. Of course, many people would just give up because they know that they won't be accepted. Here is a question: How can they know? Most of the time, they just doubt their own abilities. If you have been working on yourself, then you should not doubt your own abilities. There is a saying: *An unfired shot is a missed shot*. Basically, when you are given an opportunity to do something great, you do not need to think too much. Go for it, even though you know that your ability is not that great. Why is that? Most people are afraid of failure, but not the consequence of failure. Think about it. If you fail to get an admission into the university, what do you really lose? What really changes? Nothing. All that you lose is your time. But what if you succeed? An admission into a famous university. When you are presented with an opportunity, ask yourself: "What do I have to lose if I do this? What do I get if I do this?" And compare the pros and cons. You will see that, in most situations, you will lose so little and you have so much to gain. This way of thinking could help with your confidence as well.

It is also worth noting that you sometimes fail because of something that is outside of your own control. If you did not get that job you wanted, maybe it is because of something that gets between you and the interviewer. Try to disassociate yourself from the failure to see the problem. Maybe it is the HR's judgment, or maybe they prefer another person over you. Whatever the case, do not take failure personally. Learn from it and improve upon it. Many people take many things personally, and their confidence plummets when they receive a small criticism about their work. Even successful people receive criticism from many people. What keeps them going is the fact that they give it their best shot, and they are proud of their work.

2. During Your Speech

This part covers the period when you are actually speaking or presenting or performing something. After you have done your preparations and when you take the stage, you should feel a lot less nervous. Still, you might not feel confident in yourself while you are presenting, which could hamper your performance. So, here are a few tips to help you to look and feel confident when you are speaking.

Humor

What is a better start than to open your speech with a simple joke? When you take the stage, everyone will be quiet to listen to you. When you need to speak to more than 50 or even 10 people, you might feel the tension in the air. You can loosen that tension by telling a short joke to get the audience laughing. How does that help?

Basically, when you take the stage, you do not really see the audience as humans. Now, it doesn't mean that they are animals. Many speakers need to know that their audience is just like them. That thought alone can be enough to soothe your nervousness and help with your confidence. By cracking a short joke, you will establish that link with the audience to help you familiarize yourself with everyone in the room. Plus, by making that joke, it breaks down that invisible wall that separates you from the audience. After that laugh, many speakers say that they feel a lot less tense and they can deliver their speech properly.

Focus on Those Who Listen

When you are speaking, there will be a few reactions you will see. Some are not interested in your speech. Some people may have a knotted brow in confusion or displeasure. Some might look engrossed in your speech. While you are speaking, you should only focus on those who are interested in your speech. If you look at the people who are not interested in your speech, all you really achieve is discouraging yourself from speaking any further. Focus on the people who want to listen. You will feel that boost of confidence knowing that someone is listening, and value your words and time. As you focus on those who listen, your speech will sound more confident. That confidence will attract attention and more and more people will listen to you. Before you know it, you feel fully confident in yourself and can speak confidently. If you are having trouble speaking in a way to make people want to listen to you, then you should watch a short Ted Talk video by Julian Treasure.

Be Expressive with Your Emotions

Everyone always gets nervous when they start to speak, especially to a large audience. Some may even have a recording or themselves speaking and think that they sound and even look nervous. That alone is enough to put the confidence of many people down quickly. Sometimes, telling yourself to calm down just does not work. Anxieties are not easy to quell, but there is a different way to see nervousness. See it as excitement instead. After all, both of them stimulate us almost the same way. They turn our palms cold, they can get us a bit sweaty and jumpy, and they give us that boost of adrenaline. So, instead of feeling nervous and curl up on stage, why not take the opportunity to turn everything around and just unleash your excitement instead? It is not easy to hide your anxiety by suppression, but you can mask it under the guise of excitement. Your body will respond accordingly.

To do that, however, you need to "get into character". Basically, you need to feel your own speech. Talk passionately about everything. If you need to talk about your own disappointment, match your tone with your feelings. If you need to talk about a product, say what you are feeling about the product. Showing your own emotions is a good way to familiarize yourself with the audience, and you can even get them interested in whatever you are speaking. Instead of rehearsing and memorizing word for word (which is a bad practice), try to add your own emotional touch into your speech to give it a personality. After all, it is only logical to cater the speech to make you feel comfortable when you speak. That way, you can and will sound a lot more confident than you think.

3. After Your Speech

This covers the time after you finished speaking. Many people may think that this part is not so relevant, given the fact that you do not need to show your confidence any longer. However, this part is equally just as important since you often evaluate your own performance after your speech. If you do not handle your self-evaluation well, it will leave negative consequences on your own confidence, which will carry on to the time when you need to speak again. So, how to boost your own confidence even after you are done speaking?

Give Yourself a Pat on the Back

If you look at the people who have a low confidence, they will go down the stage with a small frown or look a bit dissatisfied with themselves. On the other hand, confident people will exit the stage with a high-five. What's the difference? The realization that they did their best.

Sure, there can be a few hiccups along the way. Everyone makes mistakes. Low-confidence people think only about their mistakes when they make them. High-confidence people look more toward their effort. No one expects you to do everything perfectly. Most people just want your best. So, instead of thinking about your mistakes, look at how many people are interested in your speech. Think of how your words influence others. Focus on the good things you have done.

Never, ever compare

All of us fall victim to this toxic habit. We always compare ourselves to other people. If you got third place in a competition, you will compare yourself to the people in the second and first place. Even if you are successful, you still compare yourself to those who are richer or more successful than you. This habit really drains you of your confidence. The thing is, you are not the other person. No one is the same. It is their path that leads them to wherever they are today. Comparison only works when two people have exactly the same history. However, that is not the case. Sure, that guy in the first place can sing better, but they probably a worse writer than you.

Instead, compare yourself to the person that you are before. You should really work on improving yourself based on the tips we gave earlier. Focus on yourself and when you notice the growth, you will become more confident in yourself. It is never healthy to compare yourself to others when you don't even know them that well.

Learn

After you went through the entire thing, give a fair evaluation of yourself. Again, disassociate yourself from the mistakes you made when you are speaking. It is not you. It is something you did. Maybe you speak too fast or too silently. Maybe you have too many "Uhms" or "Ahs". That is okay. It is in the past, and thinking too much about it will not help anyone. Instead, find ways to improve yourself. That way, when you take it to the stage once more, you will notice that you make fewer mistakes. That knowledge is definitely a confidence-booster.

Additional Tips

The tips provided earlier only cover when you need to give a presentation or when there is a large audience. However, confidence has a deeper root. You might be confident on the stage, but you might not in your private life. Unfortunately, how confident you are outside is the root of all your confidence problems. Luckily, there are many ways to improve your confidence. All you really need to do is change how you behave.

Get Off Social Media – Seriously

Social media is actually really unhealthy for your confidence. What if you log in one day and see some people taking beautiful photos of their vacation, while you struggle to even pay your bills? What if you have been single for many years, and log in only to see your best friend having yet another girlfriend? You will not feel as confident in yourself anymore.

So, unless you need to use it for business purposes, then try to limit your social media usage. In fact, social media is a cause of depression, jealousy, and other mental problems. Plus, it is a distraction. There are many ways to connect with your friends, such as the good old text messaging.

START SMALL

It is unrealistic to expect that you can be confident overnight. As we mentioned earlier, confidence is something that you need to work on. This goes hand-in-hand with knowing what you are good and bad at. By identifying what you need to work on, you can arrange them based on their difficulty one at a time. Start by doing what is necessary, then what is possible, then you will realize that you are doing something that you once thought you cannot do.

POSTURE

This applies to every aspect of your life. Stand up straight with your shoulders back. This is the first rule from the book "12 Rules for Life" by Jordan B. Peterson. Confidence does come from the inside, but certain external conditions do have an influence on it. If you change the way you stand, sit and walk by opening up, you will eventually feel that boost of confidence.

Many scientific studies have shown that the correct posture will lead to the increase in testosterone by up to 20%, and this hormone is linked to your confidence. Plus, the stress hormone cortisol also decreases by just forming a habit of having the correct posture.

You might be thinking that such a habit is hard to establish. Not really. You can start small by assuming the correct posture for about 2 minutes a day. You will feel a lot better. It really helps when you are doing a presentation with the correct posture. It makes you feel confident, and it tells others that you are confident.

EXERCISE

Just like how confidence is like a muscle, you should work on your muscles like you work on your confidence as well. Sure, confidence comes from the inside, but no one wants to look ugly. Physical fitness is one sure sign to others that you are committed to improving yourself. Plus, you would look more approachable when you look fit.

On a more primal level, your brain knows that you need to remain fit in order to escape from any danger. If you are not fit, then the brain always tells you to play it safe, whether your life is on the line or not. It is merely a habit that humans have formed for a long time, and it is not easy to shake it off. Therefore, when you are fit, your brain knows that you can escape from danger. That makes you more confidence in yourself. You do not need to pack some beefy muscles. You just need to remain fit, and there are countless guides out there to help you achieve just that.

DRESS PROPERLY

Another tip on pampering yourself is to dress well. After all, it is a sure way for others to know that you are confident in yourself. Plus, you can give your confidence a little boost when you know that you look good. Plus, you do not need to do much. Just have your clothes tailored, shower regularly, take care of your skin, and dress professionally when you go to work.

SPEND TIME WITH CONFIDENT PEOPLE

Many people underestimate the influence their peers have on them. It is worth noting that your entire life is shaped to some degree by the people you spend your time with. We talked about how your childhood can influence your confidence, but the only people you spend those tender years with are your parents. The same could be said when you were spending time with your friends during elementary school all the way to university. Your circle of friends tells others the kind of person you are. After all, you won't hang out with your friends if you are different and don't fit in well. Bird of a feather flock together. If you spend time with people who are not confident in themselves, you will inherit their trait eventually. So, start by spending time with the people you know that are confident. Learn from them, such as the way they walk, talk and think.

Smile

It's not that hard. Try to smile as much as possible. Especially when you are giving a speech but feeling a bit tense, you can release that tension with a bright smile. It works wonders on the brain because you cannot possibly smile under pressure, so you are telling your brain that everything is going to be alright when you smile. That alone is a good confidence booster when things get a bit tough.

Tidy Up Your Place

Another advice given by Jordan B. Peterson. He always tells his students to clean up their bedroom. He reasoned that, by getting up and cleaning your room, you will develop a habit of noticing a problem and fix it, no matter how meager it is. You can pick up the socks, fold your clothes, put the books back into their shelves. All those things may seem small, but when you are done, you will realize that the place is a much better place to live in. This alone makes you feel happier simply because you did something good, so it helps your confidence as well. Moreover, working in a tidy, organized room helps when you need to think and focus on your work.

Positive Reinforcement

Our brains are actually perfectly wired to thrive on positive reinforcement. As humans, we love experiencing praise and positive affirmation for our achievements. That is why when we experience a tremendous amount of love and support as children, we typically grow up to have a strong sense of self-esteem. However, when this positive affirmation had not been offered, or if we find that we are failing to receive it later in life, our sense of self-esteem can drop. Fortunately, whether or not you received it in the past, you have a powerful ability to change this story and give yourself the positive reinforcement that you need to increase your self-esteem and achieve your goals with greater ease. That's right, you can celebrate and praise yourself and directly experience success as a result!

Why Positive Reinforcement Works

Positive reinforcement teaches us that we are capable of celebrating our own successes and achievements. When we positively reinforce ourselves and others, we show that what we or they have done is good and worthy. This type of praise leads to that individual feeling accepted and appreciated by people they care about, triggering a sense of community. On a basic biological level, all of us strive to fit into the community and feel like we belong. Experiencing positive reinforcement proves to us that we are fitting in and allows us to feel loved and honored by those around us.

On an even more basic level, we are individuals who are motivated by feeling good. We will do things that help us feel good and we will avoid things that cause pain on any level. Being praised for doing a job well done either through verbal praise or through a prize of sorts teaches our mind that what we have is positive. We'll want to do more of that behavior so that we can experience more good feelings.

Many children are raised in an environment where they are either ignored for their accomplishments or are reprimanded. They may be ridiculed for their interests, or they may be devalued for not being "good enough" despite having excellent results. Any of these reactions from adults, peers, and other authority figures can result in children feeling like their successes are not enough or worse, are unimportant. As a result, they begin to feel foolish and unmotivated. Experiencing positive reinforcement may feel uncomfortable because they have never experienced it and, therefore, they may struggle to positively reinforce themselves.

Learning to positively reinforce yourself when you do something that promotes greater self-esteem is a great way to push yourself into doing even better. Although it may feel odd or unnatural at first, trust that it will begin to feel normal over time as you become used to celebrating yourself and your successes. Furthermore, it will feel a lot easier to become motivated, and you'll find that acting as your own biggest cheerleader will allow you to succeed even more. This means that you hold the power to both motivate yourself and carry out your own actions.

How Positive Reinforcement Impacts Your Brain

Positive reinforcement and achieving your goals can have a powerful impact on your brain. The science behind why positive reinforcement and achieving your goals promote a greater sense of overall health is extensive. It shows us exactly why it is important that we use these behaviors in our lives. Here is what you need to know about goal-setting, positive reinforcement, and your brain's reaction.

Having goals in and of itself creates a sense of motivation in the brain. When we have something we are working toward, our brain takes on that goal for itself. This is the first step in creating motivation for ourselves. Our brains are wired to want to "win" at everything, so any time we set a goal in place, our brain instantly goes to work looking for ways to reach that goal. This "win" is seen as a positive reward by the brain.

Despite goals being positive tools for creating motivation, the brain is actually wired to default into routines. We favor routine because it is comfortable and supports us in knowing exactly what we need, what needs to happen, and how we can create safety. When there is a routine in place, we know that there is safety on a biological level—we know where our shelter is, we know where our food is coming from, and we know how our other basic needs are being met. This is why most people struggle to set goals and actually work toward them.

Although your brain appears to be working against your success in achieving your goals, it does experience a great thrill from setting and achieving them. When we take control of our minds through mindfulness, begin working toward achieving our goals, and then actually achieve them, this sets off a positive chemical reaction. Many people report experiencing a "high" because there are so many positive endorphins flowing through their brain as a reward for achieving what it set out to accomplish. The more you practice setting goals and actually achieving them, the more your brain becomes addicted, in a sense. It enjoys the "high" so much that it becomes easier and easier for you to create new goals and set out to achieve them.

In the beginning, setting and achieving goals may not be easy because it is not a part of your routine. Your brain may not be actively aware of how much joy it will derive from "winning." However, as you carry on and begin to train your brain to achieve your goals, it will no longer be about tricking your brain because it will readily be on board and prepared to support you in accomplishing anything you set out to achieve.

How to Set Goals

A major part of being able to train yourself to set out and achieve anything is knowing how to set effective goals. When you are someone with low self-esteem and are struggling to accomplish things, having the right types of goals in place can help you experience greater success. As you begin to achieve these goals, you will begin to feel an increase in your self-esteem. As a result, it will seem possible for you to achieve even larger goals. So, in order to set effective goals that are going to boost your success and increase your self-esteem, the following are some of what you'll need to do:

TURN YOUR GOAL INTO A HABIT

The first thing that you want to do is begin turning your goals into a habit. This means that you will practice them on a regular basis, achieving them over and over again. For example, say you already drink coffee every morning but you tend to skip breakfast. If you want to set the goal that you are going to start eating a healthy breakfast every morning but haven't already chances are that this is because you do not even think about breakfast until you are already feeling hungry on your way to work. In this example, drinking your coffee is the habit and eating a healthy breakfast is the goal.

Now, if you set a reminder on your phone and you begin incorporating breakfast alongside your coffee into your daily routine, you are more likely to be successful. Because you are reminded to prepare your meal every day, you will find yourself beginning to develop it as a new habit. This will result in you creating a new, positive habit.

Science has shown that habits and goals are stored differently in the brain, so reframing a goal as a habit can make it easier for your mind to become used to the new task and integrate it easier. However, because it was still a goal, you also experience the same great rewards of dopamine and self-esteem spikes when you accomplish it.

CHANGE YOUR ENVIRONMENT

Our environment has a tendency to support us in maintaining habits and, inadvertently, can make it difficult for us to change our ways. When we are consistently in the same surroundings, it can be challenging to produce new habits or results because we are being mentally triggered by the environment that we are in. This results in us doing the same thing over and over, even if we have set out to do something different.

If you are looking to do something new in your life, try changing up your environment. This could be as simple as rearranging things or creating a new atmosphere in your home with furniture and décor, or it could be more complex such as changing where you spend your time or where you do your work. By changing your environment, you trigger your mind to see things through "new eyes," meaning it becomes easier for you to create new routines and habits.

Set Micro-Goals

As mentioned earlier in this chapter, positive rewards are a great way to support yourself in achieving your goals. When you attain a goal, your brain releases dopamine. You feel happy because you've received a positive "reward" for your success. Setting micro-goals essentially means setting a series of smaller goals that are easier and quicker to achieve. For example, set the goal to accomplish one extra task at work that day or to spend a few extra minutes scrubbing the bottom of your feet in the shower. These small yet easy-to-achieve goals are great for individuals who are in the process of building self-esteem because they allow you to quickly experience success and therefore receive regular dopamine release. As a result of feeling good about your success, your self-esteem goes up and you feel even more confident about achieving future goals. From there, you can more easily set increasingly larger goals.

HOW TO BECOME YOUR OWN BIGGEST CHEERLEADER

Cheering ourselves on is an extremely valuable tool for achieving our goals and feeling confident in ourselves. It may feel strange at first, but becoming your own biggest cheerleader is one of the greatest gifts that you can give yourself.

Because many children are not adequately supported or celebrated in their successes as youths, they have a tendency to criticize their mistakes rather than celebrate their successes. This can lead to a lack of motivation, stress, guilt, and other emotions and symptoms that represent low self-esteem. On the other hand, when you celebrating yourself and your wins no matter how small or great they are, you begin to treat yourself kindly and become capable of recognizing all that you have to offer.

As you are going about achieving new goals, give yourself pep talks and cheer on every milestone along the way. For example, let's say you have been getting out of bed at 9 AM but you now want to get out of bed at 8 AM. If you manage to wake up half an hour past 8 AM a few mornings in a row, rather than criticizing yourself for never being good enough and always doing things wrong, give yourself a round of applause for the improvement! Realize that you are already halfway toward achieving your goal and that means you have plenty to celebrate. This is a huge milestone!

Recognizing these opportunities to cheer for yourself and celebrating whenever you can is a great way to stay motivated. Aside from giving yourself pep talks, you can do this by using affirmations such as "I am doing great" or "I am already successful." You can also leave encouraging notes where you can always stumble upon them or even buy yourself a present whenever you achieve a significant milestone!

Healthy Body, Healthy Mind

Many people fail to recognize the strong relationship between our body and our mind. When we are not adequately taking care of our bodies and our physical health, our mental health will begin to deteriorate as well. Full health requires a balance of mental and physical health to keep us in our best shape and support us in feeling our best.

HOW PHYSICAL HEALTH IMPACTS SELF-WORTH

Self-worth and body image go hand in hand. When we have a low sense of self-worth, we tend to stop taking care of our bodies. Soon, they get out of shape, may become plagued with illness and chronic pain, and would otherwise no longer serve us well. Alternatively, if we lead a stressful life that prevents us from having the time to take proper care of our bodies, we begin to get out of shape and may also feel the effects of our stress as it stirs illness within the body. As a result, we become embarrassed, and we begin to experience a lowered sense of self-worth.

Our bodies, simply put, are a major part of us. They are a large piece of our identity, and they play a massive role in who we perceive ourselves to be. When we are not taking care of our bodies, we are directly telling our minds that we do not feel worthy of our time and attention. Instead, we feel that other things are more important. This lowers our self-worth, and it also begins to stimulate sensations of shame, guilt, and disappointment in ourselves. This further damages our self-esteem and self-confidence.

Another way that our physique impacts our mental health is in how we are affected by the biology of the body. An unhealthy body generally has imbalanced hormones and struggles to perform basic tasks. It results in our body producing more cortisol, the stress hormone. This is meant to kick us into gear to give us the energy needed to take better care of ourselves, but if we ignore the signs, we simply end up in a chronic state of stress. As a result, our mental health begins to suffer as well. This stress can create even lower self-worth and self-esteem in people.

The following three ways are excellent practices you can begin using right away to start balancing your body out once again and ensure that your healthy body is able to support your mental health.

Taking Better Care of Your Diet

Better health overall always starts in the gut. Your gut health is directly responsible for nearly every else in your body, from balanced hormones to proper organ function. When you are taking good care of your gut health, taking care of everything else becomes significantly easier. So how do you do that?

Proper gut health starts with a nutritious diet that is rich in everything you need to not only survive but also thrive. Eating a diet rich in color and with adequate proteins, fatty acids, and other important nutrients can support you in having stronger health in general. This means that you will begin to experience greater self-worth and greater self-esteem!

While supplements can be a beneficial way of getting important nutrients into your body, the best way to go about it is to eat a diet that is rich in what your body needs. Supplements do not tend to be broken down and absorbed by the body as easily, resulting in you simply passing many of the nutrients via urine or stool. If you do choose to use supplements in addition to a healthier diet, it is important to choose organic, high-quality supplements that will deliver the best impact on your body. You should also adjust your diet to increase your levels of healthy nutrients and vitamins.

Some things that you should begin adding to your diet to improve your overall health, specifically your mental health, include things like chia seeds, salmon, spinach, and eggs which are all rich in omega fatty acids. These acids are excellent for your brain health. Other foods include berries, nuts (especially Brazil nuts), oysters, yogurt, liver, and broccoli. These all contain high levels of vitamins like vitamins C, D, and B, protein, calcium, and other minerals. You can further increase your nutrient intake by choosing organic, pesticide-free food.

In addition to what you are eating, you should also pay attention to what you are drinking. You want to ensure that you are staying well-hydrated by drinking plenty of water throughout the day. You should avoid drinking excess alcohol or consuming too much caffeine. Keeping these two levels to a minimum will ensure that your body is functioning optimally and that it has the best chance of digesting and absorbing all of the healthy nutrients you are feeding it. Another great way to enjoy more fluids throughout the day is to make homemade juices from organic fruits and vegetables. A good, high-quality, fresh-squeezed juice is a great way to add more nutrients into your diet while keeping you hydrated.

Exercising More Frequently

Exercising is an important part of our lives that many of us tend to overlook. When we do not exercise adequately, we begin to experience the side effects of this behavior both physically and mentally. Physically, we struggle to do things that may have been easy for us at one point. Perhaps we may feel like we are not on par with our peers. It can be more of a challenge to carry things, enjoy doing activities with loved ones, or otherwise stay active and involved in others' lives when we are struggling from ill health due to lack of exercise. Low stamina and increased instances of chronic pain are just two of the many things that people with a poor exercise routine face.

Increasing your daily exercise and staying on track with a routine are great ways to increase your physical and mental health. Physically, it relieves stress from your body and helps you get back in shape. As a result, your hormone levels balance out and you begin to feel better. Your body and brain function optimally, your stress levels drop, your strong emotions dissipate in a positive way, and your capacity to face things in your day to day life increases.

Mentally, your health improves because you fccl better for taking care of yourself. Feelings of guilt and shame around having an unhealthy body begin to dissipate and you feel more confident in your ability to live the best quality of life possible. You also begin to feel sensations of pride and courage, knowing that you were able to accomplish something that previously may have felt daunting, challenging, or even outright impossible. These feelings of accomplishment and this sense of pride support you in feeling a greater sense of mental health overall.

Exercising does not need to be an extensive, hard-core workout that consumes all of your time. Instead, going for a brisk walk each day, spending a few minutes at the gym, or even doing a home workout routine in your living room are all great choices. If you are someone who is unable to work out due to a physical disability or preexisting health condition, consider communicating with your doctor to see what forms of exercise you may be able to engage in that will support you in feeling better. In many cases, there may be smaller and lower-impact things you can do such as yoga or light stretching.

The key here is not to outdo yourself or compete with anyone, unless that is what you are interested in. The key, instead, is to support yourself in achieving your own best health possible. As a result, you will begin to feel significantly better both physically and mentally.

Receiving Adequate Rest

In addition to eating right and getting enough exercise, you also need to make sure that you are getting a consistent, high-quality sleep. Rest is a highly underrated part of our daily lives, and it is typically the first to be impacted when we are feeling stressed out or unwell. We begin to find ourselves sleeping less, feeling more restless when we sleep, or otherwise not feeling fully rested when we wake. As a result, we are exhausted, and our ability to function effectively throughout the day is further impacted. Soon, we skip exercising because we are too tired. Then, we begin to continue skipping it because skipping becomes a habit. Before we know it, we are also skipping eating or eating healthy meals because we are feeling too tired to prepare them. The spiral continues until we are in a rut, feeling as though we are at our worst with a poor exercise habit, an unhealthy diet, and an even worse sleeping pattern.

Instead of letting yourself get caught in this spiral that is all too familiar for most, you can choose to pay attention to your rest and ensure that you are getting adequate sleep. Whenever you sense that you are not feeling rested enough or you are feeling too tired to do things, instead of breaking your daily routine, seek to add some extra opportunities to catch up on rest throughout the day. Take it easy by letting go of unnecessary tasks temporarily as you catch up on sleep. Go to bed a bit earlier and ensure that you practice a positive bedtime routine that will support you in having a positive sleep. Using things like chamomile, lavender, and other natural sleep aids can help you resume a restful sleep. You can also lower the lights in your house about an hour before bedtime, turn off screens, and prepare yourself for a good night's rest.

It is important that, unless absolutely mandatory, you refrain from using any chemical sleep aids. Supplements and medicines can inhibit the body's natural ability to sleep, resulting in you not being able to sleep on your own without their support. Furthermore, they can prevent you from having a truly restful sleep by manufacturing one for you. As a result, you may not feel fully rested in the morning despite having slept a long night. You may also begin to notice other unwanted symptoms that make resting and living a normal daily life a challenge. Always do your best to go natural without using any supplements or medications when it comes to sleep. If you must, consult your physician and choose the least invasive temporary method possible to ensure that it does not have a long-term impact on your sleep health.

Stay Fit and Healthy

Your overall wellbeing has a huge impact on your level of self-confidence. If you are healthy and all your systems are working properly, you can be confident. You will not only be confident because of the way you look, but also because you can think properly.

For instance, the food you eat can affect the way your brain functions. It can also affect your emotions and behaviors. Your exercise regimen can also affect your circulation, brain function, ***etc.*** Moreover, it significantly affects the way you look.

If you are overweight or obese, you are at risk of developing numerous illnesses. You can also be a target for bullies who can make your level of confidence even lower. This is why it is important to have a healthy lifestyle.

Mind What You Eat

Certain food choices can help you produce serotonin, which is a brain chemical that boosts your mood levels. When you feel positive, you become more confident to reach for your dreams and socialize better with others.

Eliminate or cut down your intake of alcohol, caffeine, fried foods and foods that contain preservatives, salts, sugars, and artificial flavorings. These food choices are not nutritious and can take a toll on your body.

Just think of it, aside from putting you at risk of various diseases, these unhealthy foods can make you fat, have breakouts or bad skin, and have dry, brittle hair among others. If you do not feel good about yourself and the way you look, you will not be confident to go out and face other people.

So the bottom line is, if you want to be more confident, you need to take good care of yourself. Make good and healthy choices when it comes to your diet.

The following foods are highly recommended if you want to improve your levels of self-confidence and self-esteem:

- Green, leafy vegetables. While all kinds of vegetables are good for your body, you should especially focus on the green, leafy variety to boost your self-confidence.

- Fruits. Bananas, kiwis, mangoes, grapefruits, and pineapples are some of your best choices when it comes to fruits that improve self-confidence. These fruits can help improve your production of serotonin.

- Herbs. Lemon balm, sage, lavender, and garlic are only some of the best herbs for improving your confidence. They have calming properties that relax your mind and body.

- Dark chocolates. When people get depressed, they usually turn to chocolates for comfort. However, if you want the healthier kind of chocolate, you should go for dark. Dark chocolates help you benefit from endorphins and phenylethylamine, which in turn produces serotonin.

- Legumes and nuts. Whenever you feel like having a snack, grab a handful of walnuts, almonds, pumpkin seeds, sunflower seeds, or cashews instead of a bag of potato chips.

Get your Body Moving

All experts agree that diet goes hand in hand with exercise. It does not matter how much you weigh or how active you are; you need to get some exercise if you want to be healthy. If you are obese or overweight, you can still exercise. You can hire a trainer to help you out. Make sure to consult your doctor before you embark on any exercise program.

Being sedentary will not do you any good. You need to stay physically active in order to get your heart pumping, burn calories, and release endorphins in your system. When you are active and happy, you can gain more confidence in yourself. You can even be more confident when you see yourself losing weight and building muscle.

Furthermore, exercising lets you avoid postural imbalances, muscle tension, and lack of energy. It makes your bones stronger and reduces your risk of chronic diseases. It also helps you regulate your blood pressure and avoid depression. Being physically healthy can do wonders for your mental health as well.

You even get to feel a sense of achievement once you reach your target weight or successfully stuck with an exercise program. Feeling good about yourself pushes you to be more confident around other people. It can help you improve your personal and professional relationships too.

Ideal Exercises to Boost your Confidence

So what exercises can you do to improve your self-confidence and self-esteem?

The American College of Sports Medicine recommends performing 26 minutes of dynamic activity that challenges the major muscle groups 3 to 5 times a week. You must also do 8 to 10 resistance exercises twice or thrice a week to improve your strength. See to it that you perform stretches at least twice a week for improved flexibility.

A lot of people have this misconception that the longer hours they exercise, the better their bodies become. This is a total mistake. It is not how much time you put into the exercise, but rather how well you do the exercise.

There is no need to spend hours at the gym or fitness center. You can get by with 30 minutes of aerobic exercises. During that time, you can release beta-endorphins into your system to make you feel better and reduce your levels of cortisol, which is a hormone linked to stress and anxiety.

Yoga is another ideal exercise for you to practice if you want to increase your self-confidence. The following poses are greatly helpful in improving your self-confidence and self-esteem:

- Forearm Plank. It builds core strength and ignites the fire center. It immediately heats up your body after just several breaths. The longer you do it, the more benefits you reap. This yoga pose activates your solar plexus chakra, which is an energy center associated to willpower, determination, and self-esteem.

- Warrior II. It is a simple pose that almost anyone can do. Even though it is simple and uncomplicated, it is still highly effective in increasing your strength and confidence. When doing this pose, imagine yourself as a warrior who is full of energy and power.

- Warrior III. Just like Warrior II, it is also effective in increasing your strength and confidence. In addition, it improves your balance and core strength. When doing this pose, make sure to take even breaths and keep your feet planted firmly on the ground.

- Half Moon Pose. Although a little bit more challenging than the previous poses, it is highly effective in cleansing your mind of self-doubt. It helps you gain more confidence in yourself. When doing this pose, make sure that you work your core with your legs to build more strength.

Social Networks

Social media is used by more than 3 billion people. It is a hugely powerful way to connect with others, support individuals in staying close with friends and family and make new ones. When used properly, social media can be a wonderful tool that enhances our daily lives. Unfortunately, most people are not practicing healthy social media boundaries and practices. As a result, many are finding themselves feeling a reduced sense of self-worth and self-esteem.

THE BENEFITS OF SOCIAL MEDIA

Social media has many positive aspects that can enhance our daily lives. From giving us a method of communication with loved ones to keep us connected no matter how many miles separate us, social media can have a beautiful impact on our world.

One way that social media is truly great at is in connecting us with people all over the world. Through various methods, we are able to connect with like-minded individuals no matter how far apart we are geographical. This is the first time in history that we have been able to create friendship circles that do not have to consider borders or barriers because we have access to all of the tools that we need to support friendships across the world. This can lead to a great mental boost by helping individuals find others who they can connect to in ways that may not be possible when interacting with others in person. This can also lead people to find support groups filled with people who understand the traumas or adversities that they have faced in their lives.

Another great benefit of social media lies in its ability to instantly update virtually everyone with information regarding current events, news, and other information. In the case of natural or man-made disasters, this can be a powerful tool for informing everyone about the event and for giving individuals the opportunity to instantly let loved ones know if they are safe.

For business owners, social media offers a fantastic opportunity for them to market and share their products and services with people all across the world. It can support them in accessing a global market that may have otherwise been off-limits for them. Previously, accessing the global market required a large budget to support individuals in being able to access, communicate with, and send their products. Now, you can simply hop on social media, share images, and ship when someone orders.

Lastly, social media is known to be great for anyone seeking genuine fun and entertainment. With many pages devoted to sharing jokes, fun and inspiring videos and other enjoyable content, it can be pleasant to hop online and see what the latest viral trends are. From silly animal videos to delicious recipes, there is something to be found for everyone.

Social Media and Self-Esteem

One extremely negative impact social media can have on us is creating an unhealthy level of self-esteem. Our fear of not being "good enough" due to having constant access to information of people who appear to be doing "better than us" can result in massive issues with our mental health and self-esteem. Often, we struggle to realize that everyone is only sharing the highlights of their lives. Furthermore, we are seeing many people's different highlights. It can quickly appear like everyone else is better because their house looks better, their bodies look better, their families look better, their images are better, they have more than we have, they are wealthier than we are, or whatever other false beliefs we begin to tell ourselves. The reality is that when we do this, we are comparing ourselves to completely outrageous standards.

If you are seeing everyone's highlight reel but no one's real life, two things happen. First, it can begin to look like someone has their whole life together just because you saw one image they posted that looked well-put and joyful. Because you have been scrolling through everyone's highlights, you may not actually realize that this was the first picture like that which this person had posted and they otherwise look "normal." As a result, everyone's highlights combine and become one super standard that no human could live up to.

Secondly, you never actually know everything that someone else is dealing with. Though their life may look great online, you have no idea what they are facing in real life. Posting on social media may be their outlet to support them in feeling happy and free from an otherwise difficult life. Alternatively, they may not be facing any challenges at this time in their life but you are; thus, you begin to compare your difficult time to their seemingly easy one. We often mistake this as believing that they never face challenges. In reality, we all do.

Comparing ourselves to people online—being regularly exposed to images of people who are doing things "better" than we are based on our perception—can be extremely damaging to our mental health. We can quickly begin to feel like we do not fit in or belong or like we are doing something fundamentally wrong that is preventing us from being able to be "as good as they are." This results in extremely low levels of self-esteem, harsh self-talk, and behavior that can be extremely damaging to your wellbeing.

Beyond comparison, some individuals actually experience regular instances of cyber abuse and peer pressure online. Being exposed to individuals who nitpick and act rude about everything we post can be extremely painful, further lowering our self-esteem and self-confidence. While many believe that this only happens to youths, the reality is that it can happen to anyone. Some of us may have an unkind or overly critical family member or friend, for example, who seems to enjoy pestering us about everything. While this may be manageable at the occasional dinner or get-together, having it happen every time you post something online can be damaging to your overall health. Furthermore, you may feel a sense of conflict as to whether or not they are permitted to continue holding space on your social media platform. You may not want to delete them for fear of being seen as rude, which can lead to you keeping them around and receiving even more damage from them. It is important to realize that you are always entitled to keep your online space safe for your mental health and that bullying or peer pressure in any form is never acceptable. You are always entitled to cut off people who are treating you unkindly.

Unhealthy Social Media Practices

Few of us are taught how to use social media without abusing it. As a result, many of us are guilty of following people who make us feel poorly about ourselves or who do things that are beyond our capability. For example, let's say you are seeking to become healthier and you follow several personal fitness buffs for motivation. However, virtually none of them look how you look when you are at your best personal fitness. Following these people can be dangerous for you. If you are not practicing proper mindfulness, you may begin to compare yourself to these individuals and feel extremely disappointed in yourself when you do not look like them. This can result in you wondering what is wrong with yourself; you may become your own biggest bully. To prevent such dangers, it is important to steer clear of those who set unreasonable and impossible expectations for their friends and followers. Instead, follow people who are healthy motivations and who encourage you to be your best self. This can support you into having a healthy motivation as well, without constantly comparing yourself to people who have a body type that is wildly different from yours.

Another thing that people tend to do on social media is spending far too much time on it. "Information overload" is a real issue that people are beginning to face on the daily. Constant access to so much information is stressful and can result in you struggling to actually digest or act on any information. Even if you are following people for inspiration, getting too many pieces of advice on how to improve yourself can result in you not knowing where to start and feeling too overwhelmed to actually begin. As a result, you may find yourself procrastinating because you are struggling to find a starting point and to follow actual, reasonable steps forward. Furthermore, some of this information may be conflicting since there is rarely one single right way to achieve anything.

Social media has also been shown to create lowered self-esteem in individuals who substitute online interaction for in-person interaction. If you feel it is easier and more enjoyable to stay up-to-date with people on social media rather than meeting with them in person and sharing proper time together, you may eventually find yourself avoiding people altogether. As a result, your social skills will begin to deteriorate, and it may begin to feel even more challenging to actually communicate with other people. And when you find that you need to communicate in person, it may feel difficult to know what to say or how to behave because your usual interactions are typically done online.

Lastly, social media can lead to unhealthy habits like distraction and procrastination and to avoiding healthy lifestyle habits like eating, exercising, and sleeping. This can lead to you putting things off, refusing to actually get involved in your life, and finding yourself struggling due to poor mental and physical health. It has been shown that many people who spend an excessive number of hours on social media also tend to have poor exercise routines, an unhealthy diet, disrupted sleep, and a tendency to put things off until later as they distract themselves further. This can lead to a negative cycle that deteriorates important things like self-esteem, self-confidence, and mental and physical health.

Healthy Social Media Practices

Just because social media can have a negative impact does not mean it is inherently bad. In fact, social media can actually be incredible. However, it is important that you practice healthy social media engagement when you use it. Using proper methods to respect social media and having healthy boundaries can support you in gaining all of the benefits without suffering a negative impact on your general wellness.

The first thing you need to do is to keep your timelines clean and positive. Ensure that you are not friends with or following individuals who set unreasonably high standards for their friends or followers, or who bully or pressure others. Although it may feel uncomfortable to unfriend or unfollow some people for fear of hurting their feelings, it is important to your own health that you not keep these individuals in your immediate space. This can protect you from their damaging effects. If you do follow people for motivation and inspiration, make sure that these people are positive and all-inclusive. Attempting to be motivated and inspired by people who only see the world one way is challenging and may further result in self-esteem issues.

You should also make sure that you are not using social media for too long. Spending too much time online will lead to information overwhelm, resulting in you feeling too weighed down to actually participate in a normal and healthy life. It can also lead to distraction and procrastination. If you are spending so much time online that you find you are not engaging in a healthy lifestyle, it may be time to limit your time online and ensure that you are staying motivated to actually do what you need to in order to live a happy life. Get exercise, eat healthy, sleep plenty, and make sure that you are keeping up with all of your physical needs.

Lastly, ensure that you are also spending time engaging in healthy in-person relationships with people. Substituting in-person relationships for online relationships can have a negative impact on your social skills, resulting in lowered self-confidence and self-esteem. Plan regular activities with friends, go to social engagements and regularly network in-person so that you can continue to practice healthy social skills and feel more confident in yourself and in the connections you make with others.

Connect with Yourself

One of the features of someone who has a healthy self-esteem is a clear understanding of who they are. So, naturally, connecting with yourself and getting to know yourself on a deeper level is a great way of getting to know who you are and increasing your self-esteem. After all, it is hard to represent yourself and have confidence in yourself if you are not entirely clear on who you are and what you are representing!

Connecting with ourselves is not something that modern culture allows a lot of time for. However, if you take your time and do it strategically, you can begin to connect with yourself on a deep level through everyday activities. In this chapter, we are going to explore how you can cultivate your skills, accept compliments, and practice self-compassion.

CULTIVATE YOUR SKILLS

Feelings of incompetence have the ability to drive our self-esteem lower and leave us feeling incapable and unworthy. When you take the time to cultivate your skills, you give yourself the opportunity to get to know yourself through the skills that you are cultivating. You also begin to feel more competent and confident in your ability to use those skills because you have spent time practicing and refining them.

When you are looking to boost your self-esteem, you should focus on cultivating your social skills, as well as any skills that will serve you in what you do on a day-to-day basis. For example, say you have an interest in painting. Spending time cultivating your painting skills by attending classes, practicing in your spare time, and studying the art, in general, will support you in feeling more confident about this skill. Alternatively, say you feel very shy and lack confidence around new people. Spending time learning how to interact with strangers, break the ice, and establish friendships is a great way to cultivate social skills that will allow you to feel more confident in new environments.

There are many ways that people can work toward cultivating their skills. Spending time in classes, studying and reading up on the skills, and actively practicing them are all important.

Putting yourself in environments where these skills are used frequently and giving yourself the space to begin practicing them are excellent ways to start as well. You can also begin spending time around people who have this skill and with whom you feel comfortable admitting that you do not yet feel confident in it. When you befriend and spend time with people who understand and have compassion and empathy for beginners and who are willing to share knowledge with you, it gives you a great opportunity to learn even more. There is a saying that goes "If you are the smartest person in the room, you are in the wrong room." Follow this wisdom by ensuring that you are surrounded by people who have varying degrees of knowledge on the skills you want. This is a great way to expose yourself to different perspectives, pieces of wisdom, and knowledge.

Another area where many people feel a lack of confidence is in their life skills. Perhaps you struggle to cook well or you do not know how to do laundry; perhaps you are ineffective at cleaning, you are poor at making routines and sticking to them, or you lack other important life skills—if any or all of this sounds like you, spending time learning to cultivate these life skills can go a long way to support you in growing your self-esteem. In our culture, we are taught that adults should know and do certain things in order for their status as adults to be "approved.". However, not many are taught all of these skills in their youth. Some are raised by parents who do it all for them, and others are raised by parents who also have poor life skills. This can lead to feelings of low self-esteem—if you are incapable of doing even the most basic things, doing the more complicated things in life may seem insurmountable for you. This is simply not true, and it is never too late to learn basic life skills.

If you were raised without knowing how to do these seemingly basic things, the first thing to do is to let yourself off the hook. Not knowing how to do these things does not mean there is anything fundamentally wrong with you. It simply means that you need to start practicing! There are many online guides, classes, and even in-person classes that are filled with knowledge for you to access, eventually allowing you to acquire these skills.

Taking advantage of these can help you learn more about yourself through the practice while also allowing you to feel more competent and confident. You would be surprised at how much this can raise your self-esteem!

ACCEPT COMPLIMENTS

Many people have a difficult time accepting compliments given to them by others. This is not only a sign of low self-esteem, it can actually lead to even lower self-esteem in and of itself. When we deflect compliments, not only do we show others that we are lacking self-esteem, we also directly tell ourselves that we do not agree with the compliments being given to us. This deflection can prevent us from recognizing what we are good at, thus causing us to consistently feel like we are not good enough. Furthermore, the feelings we derive from the deflection can reduce our self-esteem even more. Because we are now showing others that we are feeling insecure and weak, we feel worse and our self-esteem plummets further.

Accepting compliments when you have low self-esteem can feel challenging, maybe even impossible. You may be wondering why other people are recognizing positive things about you, perhaps leaving you feeling confused or frustrated. You might also experience emotions like embarrassment, uncertainty, disagreement, and discomfort. This is because you likely do not see yourself in the way they describe; therefore, it is a challenge for you to accept that other people might see you this way. When you deflect it, you do not give yourself the chance to begin seeing the amazing things in yourself that other people are obviously recognizing. This means that you may be keeping yourself stuck on the treadmill of "not good enough," because you are not accepting that you are.

While you should never rely on compliments as a way of determining your self-worth, having the capacity to accept them is important. Ignoring compliments obviously leads to distress and more struggles with your self-esteem. Embracing and accepting them, however, is a tool you could use to build your self-esteem. It does so by allowing you to actually accept and embrace the positive things about yourself. As a result, you begin training your mind to see what you are actually good at. This can support you in recognizing your worth and identifying that you are good enough and that you are capable.

The next time you receive a compliment from someone, give yourself the chance to accept it. Say "thank you" and mean it sincerely. Acknowledge the compliment—affirm it to yourself. Fully embracing the compliments that you are given is a great way to begin recognizing how great you really are. If you notice you are struggling to receive compliments even though you are making a conscious effort to try, consider digging more into why that is. Spend some time understanding what is keeping you uncomfortable and why you are struggling to allow others to say nice things about you while you fully accept these compliments. You may discover that there is a story lingering inside that encourages you to reject these compliments, thus making it more challenging for you to embrace them. When you give yourself time to understand these aspects of yourself and heal them, you give yourself the opportunity to know yourself better. Then, not only will these old stories that have been keeping you blocked be solved, you will also leave yourself open to being able to receive compliments more wholeheartedly. This can lead to you having even greater success in building your self-esteem and learning how to genuinely accept and embrace other's opinion of you.

Practice Self-Compassion

A surprising number of people struggle to experience self-compassion in their lives. While we tend to have a great deal of compassion and understanding for other people and their struggles, we are known for holding ourselves to much higher standards. Then, when we struggle to meet these standards, we find ourselves feeling frustrated, embarrassed, and low. This can result in reduced levels of self-esteem, among other things that can keep us feeling down and out. Instead of being so hard on yourself and becoming hostile or rude toward yourself when you make a mistake, consider practicing self-compassion.

Self-compassion does not come naturally to most people but learning how to give yourself a break and cut yourself some slack can have a great impact on your mental health. Knowing how to accept that you are human and that it is natural for you to make mistakes or endure learning curves is important. It supports you in giving yourself the space that you need in order to feel confident enough to expand your skills, manifest your desires, and create whatever you want in your life.

The truth is, adversity can rarely be overcome with ease. It always takes time and practice for people to learn new things and move forward in their lives. When we face hardships, we need space to heal. When emotions become big and challenging, we need the opportunity to dig into them and nurture ourselves. Robbing ourselves of these needs through a lack of self-compassion would only result in us feeling even worse. We carry around burdens, feelings of lack, and a sense of being unable to do what we desire to do. This can weigh anyone down. Knowing how to release these burdens and advance forward is important.

A good way to begin practicing self-compassion is to practice optimism. You should also begin learning how to forgive yourself and how to say the words "It is okay" to yourself in the mirror. Understanding how to accept yourself as you are at each moment is key. The reality is, no one can be completely great all the time. We all make mistakes, we all deal with emotions, and hardships arise in everyone's lives. Having the capacity to accept that this is a reality of life and to love yourself through it all is essential.

You can also begin practicing self-compassion by getting to know yourself and developing rituals to support you during various situations. For example, say you are going through a challenging disagreement with a family member and you are feeling angry. Devise a ritual that allows you to dig into and understand that anger and then release it in a natural but healthy way—through art or by working out, perhaps. Knowing yourself enough to know your needs and loving yourself enough to actually take the time to fulfill them is important. This is one of the highest levels of self-compassion you can practice, and it will support you in being able to accomplish anything you desire in your life. If you are unsure of how to go about with your self-care and self-compassion rituals, the best way to start is to ask yourself this one simple question: "What do I need right now, and how can I fulfill that need?"

Quick Boosts to Self-Esteem

Rituals are a great and powerful way to boost self-esteem, but sometimes, we need a quick boost throughout the day to keep us going. Perhaps you are generally someone who has great self-esteem but you need an extra push for something important, such as a business meeting. Maybe you are still learning how to have great self-esteem and you want to really lift yourself up before meeting with a new friend. Either way, it is essential to know how to boost your self-esteem in a pinch. This will support you in feeling confident and capable of achieving anything it is that you are about to face.

These activities can be accomplished as a part of a daily self-esteem boosting ritual, or they can be used to amplify your self-esteem on any particular day or for any specific event. Having these activities in your self-esteem toolkit is a great way to make sure that you can boost yourself up for anything, anytime. Be sure to practice them regularly so that you can begin experiencing benefits and learn how they work for you. That way, when you need them in a pinch, you'll know exactly what to do and you'll already feel confident in using them.

Power Poses

Power poses are a great tool to use to boost your self-esteem. These are specific poses that are meant to be done in front of a mirror, as seeing yourself in these poses is said to give a massive boost to your self-esteem. However, you can also practice them without a mirror should one not be available when you need it. These poses are designed in a way that allows you to see yourself exercising confident body language. That way, the same reaction you get when you see someone else practicing confident body language is triggered. Because you begin to associate this feeling with yourself, it becomes easier for you to recognize yourself as the confident one. Thus, your self-esteem increases and you feel more confident around others as well.

One of the most popular power poses to use includes standing in front of a mirror with your feet stretched out a bit past shoulder width and your arms raised up in a "V" above your head, with your hands in fists. This pose is sometimes called "The Performer," and it is known to help boost your confidence and self-esteem by making you feel like a winner. Since you look like you are in the winning circle, it becomes easier for you to feel like you are someone with great confidence. This pose should be practiced for at least 30 seconds, but it is often recommended to hold it for an entire minute to get the most out of it. It is amplified by repeating affirmations to yourself while you hold the pose.

Puffing out your chest with your hands on your hips and your feet hip-width apart is another great power stance. When we stand in this position, we get the feeling that we are ultra-confident and that we are in charge. It is almost like a superhero pose when they are proud of accomplishing what they set out to do. Standing in this pose in front of the mirror for 30-60 seconds while repeating affirmations to yourself is a great practice. You can also use it in action in any situation where you need increased confidence. For example, when you are talking to your boss, you can use this pose. Try not to be too obvious or awkward about it, but hold it strong and firm. This way, you can assert your confidence externally through your pose while also increasing your confidence internally through it. This will support you in appearing more confident while also feeling more confident.

Another pose you can do is often called the "Superman Pose." This one can be done in front of your mirror for 30-60 seconds. You do it by simply standing in front of the mirror with your feet hip-width apart, one hand on your hip and one stretched above your head in a fist. You can then puff up your chest a bit and tilt your chin upward. Standing in this pose can make you feel invincible and powerful, thus supporting you in feeling like you can do and accomplish anything you set out to accomplish.

Power poses are great tools that can be used in a short period of time to support you in having a greater sense of confidence. While most are meant to be done in front of a mirror or in the comfort of your own space, some can be done while you are actively in conversation to help you feel more confident at the moment. These are great to use when you are beginning to feel your self-esteem diminish as they can produce a body-to-mind reminder that you are confident, capable, and worthy. Knowing how to use your body to communicate this to your mind can be extremely supportive in helping you feel more confident in action.

POSTURE

How we carry ourselves not only says a lot about who we are but also has a huge impact on how we feel about ourselves. People who carry themselves in a long, drawn-out way or who try and minimize or shrink their appearance through their posture are often seen as unapproachable and unconfident.

Recognizing your posture and understanding what it says not only about you but to you is important. If your posture is minimized and shrunken down, there is a good chance that this is because you are feeling anxious and shy about the situation you are in. This is a great indicator of low self-esteem and self-confidence. Recognizing this behavior in yourself is a great way to begin seeing how you are communicating to yourself and to others that you lack confidence. If you really tune in, it can also tell you what is causing this feeling within you. The moment you feel your posture switch from a confident and able posture to a shy and minimized one, you can begin identifying what the trigger was and why it caused your self-esteem to diminish. If your posture is always like this, it may be because you have felt low self-esteem for so long that you are struggling to feel confident in any situation.

Auditing your own posture is a great way to identify this information, but it could also give you the opportunity to adjust it. That way, you can begin consciously holding a stronger and more confident posture that conveys to yourself and others that you have a healthy self-esteem and a great sense of confidence. Doing so requires just a small amount of understanding in how your body language and posture are perceived by yourself and others.

In general, a healthy sense of self-confidence results in people having what is considered to be a healthy posture. This includes a tall, straight spine, a chin that is slightly turned up, feet that are firmly planted, and hands that are relaxed or strategically placed somewhere on the body; for example, with your hands on your hips, your arms casually by your side, or even crossed in front of you if you are feeling serious and in-charge. You should also keep your shoulders back and your chest slightly puffed forward. This is considered to be both a healthy posture and a confident one. When we hold ourselves tall and proud, we convey that we are feeling tall and proud. This then communicates to our minds, helping us to actually feel more confident and proud as well.

Wardrobe

How we dress also has a major impact on how we feel and how we present ourselves. When we are dressed poorly, we tend to feel the same. For examplc, if you are wearing baggy, ill-fitting, or uncomfortable clothes that you do not feel good in, you are not going to feel confident either. You will end up feeling frustrated, self-conscious, and maybe even invisible, depending on what you are wearing. None of these feelings add up to feeling confident or having a healthy level of self-esteem.

Wearing clothes that fit you and that genuinely feel good are important. You want to wear clothes that are comfortable against your skin, that fit well, and that has a style that genuinely makes you feel confident and proud. When you wear clothes that make you look good, you feel better wearing them. You no longer spend time fussing over yourself in the mirror or feeling self-consciousness due to a fear of not looking right, not being noticed, not visibly fitting in—you stop thinking there's something wrong with your wardrobe that could cause embarrassment. Instead, you can focus on other things.

If you currently have a wardrobe that does not make you feel like you can confidently assert yourself in any situation, you need to begin changing up your wardrobe! Having comfortable lounging clothes is important, but make sure your entire wardrobe does not consist of these. Furthermore, do not choose clothes only based on their labels. If it does not feel right for you, don't buy it. Instead, aim to create your desired look: match what looks and feels right for you. For example, say you want to look professional but you dislike blazers. Instead, you may discover a great style of blouse or dress shirt that fits you well and makes you feel more confident. Then, instead of filling your wardrobe with well-fitting blazers that make you look at yourself in disgust or frustration, you can fill your wardrobe with well-fitting blouses or dress shirts that make you feel confident and proud.

Having a strong wardrobe means that it should include pieces for every occasion. Having the right piece of clothing for any kind of situation will ensure that you'll always be dressed your best—and in a way that makes you feel great each time.

If you are unsure of how to dress yourself to feel and look great, you might consider hiring a stylist. Consulting someone who can support you in deciding what outfit will work and how you can feel amazing in it is a great way to build a wardrobe that will boost your self-esteem. Furthermore, it can be helpful if you have never shopped for this purpose before and have no idea what to purchase for yourself. Additionally, having a stylist cheer you on and tell you how great you look in your new pieces may be just what you need to feel confident in rocking them after the purchase. It can help ensure they do not go on to hang in your closet unused due to your fear of wearing them as a result of low self-esteem.

Assertiveness

Asserting yourself is not always easy, but it is essential. Those who lack self-esteem struggle to assert themselves and thus find themselves feeling underrepresented and taken advantage of in many different situations. If people do not know what you are thinking and are unaware of how passionately you feel about certain things, they are not going to be able to take you seriously. Furthermore, some people simply do not know how to take others seriously unless they are pressured into doing so by the other person's assertiveness. Knowing how to assert yourself will not only help others take you seriously, it will also help you know how to be taken seriously.

People who are not used to being assertive may have a misguided view of what assertiveness is. This often comes from fear and misunderstanding. Many who do not actively practice asserting themselves may wrongfully believe that doing so means being rude and arrogant about your thoughts and beliefs. This is not at all true. While asserting yourself can be done in a loving and kind way, it should still have a powerful and positive impact. The purpose of asserting yourself is not to be loud and obnoxious, but rather to be firm and unwavering. You want to make sure that people are aware of how you feel and that they understand that you will continue to assert yourself until they understand or listen.

Asserting yourself is important in having your needs met as well as in having your voice and thoughts represented when they need to be. For example, let's say that in a relationship, you dislike it when someone is late without giving you a heads up. If you never assert that this is not okay for you and that you dislike waiting, especially without warning, then the other party will never know and will never be compelled to change their ways. Alternatively, they may know if you have spoken up once or twice, but they may not take you seriously because you do not back it up with strength.

Now, let's say that you clearly told them how you disliked it that they're late. You then state that in the future, you will simply not wait. After that, you actually go ahead and leave the next time they do it. They will surely realize from this sequence of actions that you are serious. This is asserting yourself.

Another great scenario where you can gain value by asserting yourself is in the professional setting. Say, for example, that you are in a board meeting. The board is about to do something that results in you having to take on more work, but you are not able to reasonably handle that work in your schedule. Having the ability to assert that you are not okay with taking on this added work and asserting your alternative solution is a great way to make sure that you are not taken advantage of and that your needs and the company's needs are still met. Knowing how to assert yourself can come in handy on many occasions. Standing firm for yourself and for your truth is crucial, so be sure to practice doing it. The more you practice assertiveness, the more comfortable and natural it will become to do it, wherever and whenever you need to.

Dress With Confidence

What you choose to wear definitely alters the way you approach the world and interact with other people. If you wear something that something that you associate with powerful women, you are more likely to feel powerful and confident. What you wear does affect the mental and perceptive processes of the brain and this a proven scientific fact. Selecting a color that really brings out your best physical features or a cut of pants that accentuates your small waist, can really uplift your spirits and your confidence.

Play around with colors and find out which colors really look amazing on your and which really do nothing for your skin tone or eye color and your hair color. If you wear a color that really brings out all your best physical features, you will feel more confident from the start.

Know and understand your body shape. Dress to flatter your curves or lack thereof. Dressing in attire that really accentuates your figure can be the confidence boost you really need.

Know your strengths and use them to your advantage. Pay extra special attention to your body and really be honest about your strengths and shortcomings. For instance a curvier figure may look much more attractive in a dress that a pants suit and this should be used to your advantage. An outfit that plays to your strengths, in the perfect color and suits your body shape will have you stepping out in confidence and nothing will stand in your way.

First and foremost, make sure you are completely comfortable in what you are wearing. Add your own personal flair to your outfits, one that really puts into visual aspects what you character is and who you are. Of course if you are eccentric, this may not be the route to follow for a business meeting. Tone it down a little but definitely include something that screams you in the outfit. Your clothes are the first thing people see when they meet you and they should be able to judge your personality from the start. Most important is feel comfortable and confident in how you step out into the world.

Dress appropriately for the occasion. Overdressing or under dressing for an occasion will not encourage confidence in you. Wearing inappropriate clothing can have you cowering in a corner, afraid to say anything or make your presence known for fear of ridicule. Save yourself having to endure such an event and really take careful care when selecting your outfit. You want to feel comfortable stepping out and voicing your opinions and really taking part in discussions.

Be completely sure that the outfit you have selected allows you to feel comfortable and at ease. Showing more skin than normal may leave you feeling vulnerable whereas showing less skin than normal can leave you feeling frumpy. You should always feel comfortable and confident to step out in the outfit you have selected. It really shouldn't leave you feeling anxious at all.

Allow your time a few extra minutes in the morning to get your outfit perfectly right and step out your front door glowing with confidence and that go-getter attitude you need to succeed.

How you dress says a lot about you as a person. It will give vital indicators to what your personality type is as well as pointing out your own quirky characteristics. Dressing to suit your body completely and to highlight your strengths and hide your shortcomings, will really leave you no alternative but to feel confident and comfortable and your body language will surely reflect that in your daily undertakings. Dress for the success you deserve and allow others to see in you what you know you are capable of.

Don't try to dress in a way that doesn't allow you the freedom to express yourself and your personality. On meeting you, people want to know whether you are bold and outspoken or daring and creative and your clothes are the perfect way to showcase these features.

FABULOUS & EASY WAYS TO BOOST YOUR SELF-CONFIDENCE

Confidence is your personal weapon, your weapon against your fears, your self-doubt and an amazing tool to use in order to master skills you never though you could. Your confidence, like a muscle, needs exercise and the more you train and use it, the stronger it will become.

Besides your body language and your dress sense, there are so many ways that you can use that muscle everyday and create a more confident you, the one you deserve to be.

- Learn, learn as much as you can, learn new things. Knowledge is power and the more you know about a variety of subjects, the more confident you will feel speaking openly without the fear of being ridiculed.

- Stop paying so much attention to yourself, sometimes people tend to over think things and end up creating scenarios that really don't exist. Divert your attention to others and how you can help them. You will feel a sense of satisfaction at doing something wonderful and this will really lift your spirits and boost your confidence.

- Daily exercise is necessary for a clear mind. The psychological effects of exercise are amazing and just a short session each day will leave you feeling rejuvenated and ready to take charge. As your body becomes accustomed to the exercise and you are able to push yourself more, you will begin to notice physical changes as well and these will definitely have a positive effect on your confidence.

- Rid yourself of negativity in your life. Make a list of things that you are enduring and putting up with and make a decision to eradicate them from your life. Physically list ways to remove them and tick them off as you progress. The less negativity around you, the more positive your outlook and the more confident you will feel.

- Learn to recognize and appreciate your achievements. If you are unable to appreciate and acknowledge what you have done, how can you possibly expect anyone else to. Remember that the line that borders egotistical is fine and that is not a quality you want to portray.

- Branch out and spread your wings. Social events are a wonderful way to meet new people. Yes, it may be unnerving striking up a conversation with a complete stranger but with the right attitude, you may find a friend for life. Take a chance and exercise that confidence muscle.

- Stop placing yourself in little boxes or pigeonholes of how you think people expect you to act. Who cares! Do what makes you happy and be yourself, what other think of you is not your problem, it's theirs.

- Don't allow yourself to begin a negative thought pattern where you tell yourself you can't do something or you'll never be able to, it is hard as we all have these thoughts, just give yourself a gentle reminder that these negative thoughts are not food for your confidence and make a concerted effort to change the pattern.

- Make deliberate decisions regarding things that really matter to you. It is so easy to fall into a pattern where you just go with the flow in order to maintain peace and harmony but at the end of the day, you are the one who is left feeling unsatisfied and unhappy. Make your own decisions and stick by them no matter what anybody else says.

- Don't be afraid! This is the key to happiness and confidence. If you are always afraid that you will look stupid or silly, you will never truly try anything to your full potential. Speak up, act out and don't worry about how you seem to others.

- Everybody possess degrees of self-confidence, you just don't realize it. Pay more careful attention to the times when you make decisions, speak out or act out, where you don't second guess yourself. Pay attention to how that feels and make a concerted effort to apply those principles and feelings to times when you do second-guess yourself. That feeling of doing or saying something without doubt is a feeling you will want to hold onto and carry through other areas of your life.

- Recognize your doubts, take heed and let them go. Everybody is human and you will at some time or another, feel doubt over an action or a decision you have made. Try to understand why you feel that doubt and use them to your advantage as you move forward in life.

- There is no rule book in life. All the "you shouldn't", "you can't" and "don't do's" are hindering you from being you. Once you discard these rules, you will feel free to make decisions based on you and your thoughts and feelings and not based on society's guidelines.

- Yes, you lost out on something because you were to afraid to go through with it. There is no use pondering over this loss. Be honest with yourself and perhaps you will make a different decision next time.

- Everybody gets scared sometime in life. Nobody has experienced everything and mastered everything. Allow yourself to feel scared, this is not a sign of lack of confidence, it merely means you are stepping out into unexplored waters and it is a new experience. Fear is normal, embrace it and use it to your advantage. Fear shows you that you are about to take a growth leap in your confidence and grow as a person, don't run away, face it head on and give it all you've got.

- There will always be people in your life that put you down or belittle you. Don't stand for this any longer. Let these people know in no uncertain terms that you deserve better than what they are doing and you expect better. Their own fears should not be projected onto you.

- Life is full of twists and turn and yes there will be good and there will be bad. Embrace all the experiences as these are the tools you will use going forward. The good are encouragement to continue on that path and the bad are reminders of decisions that you could have made differently. These experiences make us who we are so there is no use hiding from them.

- When things get tough and you feel as if you can't cope. Stop! There is no situation that you are not strong enough for and you need to keep telling yourself that no matter how hard it gets along the way. Think of the elation you will feel when you finally battle your way through and make it out in one piece.

- Leave the drama for the soap operas. There are more important things in life to consider and spend your time on and you should put more effort into these meaningful exercises.

- Don't sell yourself short. Avoid taking the easy way out of situations. The lessons you learn on the long, hard route can not be measured and you will develop and grow as a person through these trial and tribulations. The easy way out may give instant gratification but at the end of the day, the reward will not be as satisfying.

- Be confident enough to admit when you are wrong. Admitting you are wrong does not mean you are weak or silly, it simply means that you have the courage to change your mind once all the relevant information has been presented. Don't become stubborn and insolent in order to stick to a decision which you realize was the wrong one, this isn't confidence, it's stupidity and arrogance.

- Trying to do everything on your own is not always a viable option. Have the confidence to admit that you need assistance and ask for it. You will be admired for you approach in getting the task completed properly. Being confident doesn't mean you have to go it alone.

- Surround yourself with people who support you and encourage you in everything you do. The positive attitude will feed your confidence. Steer clear of those who seek to belittle you or put you down, the negative attitude will only cause you to creep further into the shell you are trying to escape.

- There is really no point in battling and fighting against things in your life that make you unhappy. Accept them, embrace them, learn from them and move on to happier pastures.

- Your body mirrors your minds attitude. Outwardly display confidence and the psychological affects will astound you. Keeping your body in a positive state will encourage your mind into that state as well and the more your mind believes, the more your body will show the benefits.

- Be completely happy with who you are, what you believe in and the talents you have. Stop comparing yourself to everyone else, we were all made with different features and special characteristics. Embrace yours and see the magic begin.

- The state of your environment affects the state of your mind. Keep your space organized and clutter free and allow your mind the space to perform. A clutter free space also encourages confidence, being able to find what you need, when you need it will definitely have you on the path to success. Not being able to find things amid a pile of paperwork puts you on edge and you start to doubt your own abilities.

- You are valuable on your own. Never allow your self-worth to be dependent on another person. Relationships are wonderful and rewarding but first you need to have the confidence and belief in yourself. A partner is not there to make you believe in yourself and you shouldn't need one to validate that you are worthy.

- Work on your body image. If you are unhappy with how you look on the outside, your confidence will take a beating. Work on your image, lose some weight, start a healthy eating plan, anything that makes you feel happier about yourself. A healthy body image will have you flaunting your stuff with confidence.
- Learn from confident people you trust and respect. You don't need to copy them or mirror their every move but take notice of the small things they do to display confidence and think about what you could do differently to reach that desired state.
- Yes, it is wonderful to be able to help people and take on tasks requested of you but don't feel pressured into it. If you know you can't deliver what is expected, rather decline. There is no need for you to make excuses or offer reasons for declining. Don't put yourself in a position where you may end up in hot water or end up the bad one for not doing what was asked of you.
- Everybody has strengths and weaknesses, that is the nature of being human. We can't all be perfect, what a boring world that would be. Your weaknesses can only define you if you allow them to. Embrace your weaknesses and make a concerted decision to work on them. Encourage your strengths and you will find that your weaknesses don't seem all that strong and overpowering anymore.
- Be bold and daring. Don't spend your life taking risk assessments because the important moment will pass you by. Face challenges and fears with courage and strength and you will succeed.
- Life will be full of challenges and yes, you won't always succeed the first time round but that is all part of the journey

and the learning curve we must all face in order to become who and what we were meant to.

- Accept the fact that every human being has flaws, that is what makes you human. Realize where you went wrong in a situation and evaluate how you could better have handled the situation, learn from it and move on. Nobody can say without a doubt that they are flawless and are perfect in every way. Forgive yourself and move forward.

- If you are in the wrong, accepting it and apologizing are excellent qualities. You do not however have to accept guilt for everything that goes wrong or for every problem every person you know encounters. Accept blame where it is warranted but don't roll over and take the blame for things beyond your control.

- Treat others how you would want them to treat you and how you would treat yourself. Don't use derogatory terms to identify people as this is not something you would want done to you and certainly not a name by which you would call yourself. You deserve to be treated as well as you treat others and remind yourself of this daily.

- Only you are responsible for you own feelings. Of course situations and people may affect your feelings but they cannot decide that you will feel a certain way. You are the master of your own feelings and decisions.

- As long as you are doing the best you can, that is good enough. You can't expect yourself to be everything to everyone all the time and to keep everybody happy. By doing this, the one that will suffer will be you.

- Learn to accept compliments graciously and see the positive in every comment made. Don't over think compliments received and start to put negative connotations to it, a compliment is a positive aspect and should be treated as such. Give compliments freely.

- Holding on to the past, especially the negative aspects can really create negative feelings and a negative mood. Learn to forgive and move on. Forgive those who have wronged you, including yourself. Your past must not be allowed to dictate your future and it will only control you if you allow it.

- Be honest. This is very important if you want to be someone who has self confidence. If you are honest you can never be plagued by feelings of doubt or guilt.

- Stand up for yourself and what you believe in. Show conviction and don't back down even if the majority says you are wrong. If you have done your research and have your facts straight, don't give up what you believe to follow the herd just so that you fit in.

- Your life is for living, have fun, fall in love, meet new people, take chances, be serious when the time requires it but go out and truly live your life as if it was your last day on Earth.

Building Self-esteem

Self-esteem can be defined as the image a person has of himself. It is a very important factor in determining the kinds of experiences an individual will have in life and his emotional reactions to them. A person with low self-esteem tends to feel useless and uncared for, while readily blaming himself and thinking that suffering is his or her due. He or she is the one who is actually the source of his own anguish by choosing to listen to his inner critic and wallowing in depressive and negative emotional states. To get out of this vicious cycle of self-abuse, there are various means to help a person build his self-worth.

First, an individual plagued with low self-esteem must acknowledge and accept that he is suffering from this issue. Secondly, he or she should write down his or her perceived strengths and weaknesses. Thirdly, he or she will need to think up situations where he or she has displayed such qualities and shortcomings, and then analyze his emotional states and behaviors in the respective occurrences. For example, a person who has made a mistake at work will condemn himself/herself for failing at his tasks and thus undergo negative emotional reactions like guilt, worthlessness and depression. After going through the exercise of introspection, the individual should then imagine him or herself to be a highly self-assured person or picture a self-confident colleague and reflect on how his alter self or the other person would have reacted in similar situations. Finally, he or she should seek help from his or her closest friends and family by asking them how they perceive him and what they see as his strengths and flaws. This will enable him to recognize that how he or she perceives him or herself if not in tune with reality and how others perceive him or her.

Moreover, the person with low self-esteem should learn to silence his or her inner critic and replace that voice with that of an inner motivational coach. He or she needs to develop confidence by voicing his opinions in situations where he feels he can contribute positively. The individual can also try new experiences regularly in order to boost his self-image, such as learning to play a new instrument, decorating cakes, volunteering with a charity, or joining a local sports team. Furthermore, overcoming his fears will also help increase his sense of self-achievement and self-worth. For example, a person who is afraid to tread in deep waters may persuade himself to conquer his fear and swim beyond the shallow end of the pool. New adventures and experiences will enable the person to test his or her limits and build his or her self-esteem by successfully overcoming personal mental barriers, which hindered him/her from leading a positive life.

Read/Watch Inspirational Stories

A person with low self-esteem will invariably linger in a vicious circle of negative emotions while shying away from life's opportunities. To that end, inspirational stories and movies can help alter a person's negative emotional state and cause him to question his life, attitudes and behaviors. Some stories and films are based on true life events of others who have managed to overcome their low self-worth and developed their inner strength in order to achieve their goals in life.

The Alchemist, written by Paulo Coelho, describes a shepherd in Andalusia who dreamt about an Egyptian treasure and the path he takes in order to fulfill his dream. The novel is an inspiration to many people around the world and it stresses the importance of taking the leap of faith to achieve one's dream. The shepherd makes a series of decisions which brings him closer to his goals, and the choices he makes completely transform his life. The writer carefully illustrates the protagonist's internal conflicts and how he successfully overcomes each hurdle.

Another particularly empowering book is Eckhart Tolle's The Power of Now. It deals with the importance of focusing on the present instead of lingering on past or future events. It evokes the fact that past and future moments are only occurring in a person's thoughts while he is living the present moment. It also suggests meditation and relaxation techniques to let go of anxiety and worry.

The Monk Who Sold His Ferrari, by Robin Sharma, is another inspirational book that narrates a story about a successful lawyer who gives up his fame and money in order to embark on a journey in search of himself. The book is basically about self-discovery, finding out who you really are within and what meaning you want to give to your life.

The Secret, by Rhonda Byrne, is a novel that has been turned into a short movie. It explores the law of attraction and discusses the way our thoughts influence different events occurring throughout our lives. Positive thoughts attract favorable occasions while negative thoughts lead to harmful happenings, hence the law of attraction. If you focus on things or events that you fear and hate, they will eventually manifest themselves in your lives.

Lastly, The Bucket List is a movie concerning two terminally ill men who set out on a journey to complete a list of things they wish to do before they die. The story underlines positive living, enjoying the present moment, the ephemeral nature of life and the way you should go about making your life worth living and creating memories worth remembering. There are many such inspirational movies which accentuate the importance of having a positive attitude towards life. TED videos constitute a series of genuine motivational stories about people who have managed to overcome their low self-esteem in life. To kick start your journey toward improving your self-esteem, you should consider watching or reading some, or all, of the above films and books.

Control your emotions

Emotional Intelligence is an important aspect in determining the way a person lives his life. It defines the level of self-confidence a person possesses, which will enable him to tackle day-to-day problems. According to Daniel Goleman's 'Five Pillars of Emotional Intelligence', self-awareness is a prerequisite to having high self-esteem. It consists of being aware of your emotional states and the effects they have on other people. A person should be able to identify, analyze and understand his own emotions and impulses. How a person reacts to a particular situation depends on his level of emotional awareness and his ability to control it. Another component of Emotional Intelligence is self-regulation, which is the ability of an individual to control his emotions, curb his negative impulsive responses and to think before expressing his emotions.

A person should thus learn to suspend judgment in any particular situation and think carefully before acting. For example, in a situation where an individual gets depressed because of the words uttered by someone else, the person should first be conscious that he is experiencing depression. He should then question the reason why he is in such a damaging emotional state. The next step would be to analyze his impulses and reflect upon whether his emotional reactions will be constructive or destructive. Despair is a very harmful emotion. The person needs to learn to detach himself from situations that have a negative impact on his emotional state and then develop his logical thinking skills. The individual who involves himself emotionally in all situations will tend to have extreme emotional responses. Therefore, a human being should not let a situation or another person alter his emotional state and elicit negative reactions from him.

Moreover, a person should practice controlling his or her emotions. For somebody accustomed to resorting to destructive emotional states and behaviors, it will be a challenge to change their thought processes and foster positive thoughts and emotions. For example, if an individual experiences negative feelings, like guilt or anxiety, they should first think in a rational way and view the situation objectively. Only after carefully examining the circumstances can they then give their judgment and decision.

Furthermore, empathy is another component of emotional intelligence. A person needs to understand the emotional setup of different people and treat those people according to their emotional reactions. In doing so, an individual can easily read another person's emotional state and avoid being emotionally engaged in the situation.

People who are emotionally intelligent have a better attitude and outlook on life. They perform well at their jobs and respond better to challenging situations.

Conquering Your Inner Critic

Everyone has an inner critic. This is the voice that tells you that the job you did might not have been so great after all, and that you don't look very good or shouldn't feel good about yourself. Some let the voice get too strong, and this can quickly wreck your self-esteem. It is normal to have some spells that are worse than others, but when your critic becomes the predominant voice in your head then it's time to learn how to conquer it.

The first step is realizing what your points of insecurity are. Journaling can help you pinpoint these aspects, as can gauging your mood at certain points during the day using useful scales such as the Rosenberg Self-Esteem Scale. Checking your self-esteem before a project and then again after can help you see if your work is bringing you down, or maybe your self-esteem grows after completing a household chore. Recognizing these patterns is a very important first step to owning and controlling your inner critic.

The next step is learning how to accept your flaws and let go of your failures. This sounds easy in theory, but in practice, it is actually very difficult. You may find it helpful to interrupt your thoughts midstream before they become persistent. Have a list of things you are proud of, especially things that are pertinent to the situation and that can help you when the doubts start creeping in. If you feel as though you're about to start criticizing yourself, think of the items on your list that make you proud and focus on them until the doubts start to subside.

A final step in beginning to conquer your inner critic happens when the first two steps are performed consistently and become habits. It is more of a change in your way of thinking. After applying the first two steps, the final step is somewhat self-fulfilling because you will naturally start to find the positive in what you've accomplished and minimize what you formerly saw as flaws. You'll find that the more you consciously review and assess your feelings, the more control you'll have over them. Knowing what makes you react negatively to a situation helps you realize what you need to do to avoid or fix the feelings quickly rather than dwelling on them, which is so common.

Overall, you inner critic is a stubborn nemesis that can be overcome with repetitive training to learn how to calm and quell the nagging that many of us are so used to. Exercises, such as the ones listed above, can help quiet the critic as well as increase your self-understanding. The exercises can help you become a better rounded person and will help in your everyday battle with your critic.

Practice, Practice, Practice

When looking to change your life and become the person you want to be, there is nothing like practice. Many people associate practice with just sports or education, but practice applies to every aspect of life and can be invaluable in becoming who you want to be. Nobody can change overnight and practice can be applied to every aspect of life to help you become the best version of yourself.

Practice doesn't have to be a person just repeating the same action over and over again; it can happen on paper or while playing out scenarios in your head. Lists and realizing what path one needs to follow are good ways to induce practice in your head, and think ahead to what you'll do during when confronted with a particular situation. Living through situations before they happen can be great social practice and will help you think on your feet so that you don't freeze in critical life situations.

Preparedness can be seen as a helpful form of practice. Writing out what you want and figuring out the best way to accomplish your goals is also a very good way to practice, since you can't very well physically practice the steps day after day. The writing and planning will make it seem like you have practiced in person though, as you will be prepared for many scenarios because you thought through them ahead of time. Dry runs can happen with drills if the provisions are available, or even something as simple as holding a conversation with yourself in the mirror can be helpful forms of preparing and practicing for many different situations.

When you get into the habit of practicing every day, you'll be surprised at how it can infiltrate and help other aspects of your life. Knowing that quickly going over something in your head and playing out different outcomes can help prepare you for so many different social interactions and then people will notice that you are more comfortable and confident.

Of course, sometimes practice is physical rather than mental. If you want to be a knitter, you'll knit until it becomes second nature, and that's the entire purpose of practicing both mentally and physically--to turn certain actions into muscle memory. The more you perform a task, the more naturally it comes the next time and therefore, the more of an expert you become.

Practice really does make perfect. Making sure you know what you want and then dedicating time to practice, practice, practice is the most important step in becoming an expert in whatever you'd like to be an expert in.

Using Affirmations to Change Your Thinking

Reprogramming negative thinking can be difficult, but there are techniques you can use to help you do so. One of those techniques is using positive affirmations.

What are affirmations? Webster's Dictionary defines an affirmation as "a statement asserting the existence or the truth of something." In other words, an affirmation is a statement saying "this exists" or "this is true."

Positive affirmations are positive words and thoughts that program your mind, similar to the way a computer is programmed. They help you focus on your goals or desires. Affirmations create mental pictures in your conscious mind. The mental pictures in your conscious mind then affect the way your subconscious mind works.

It's best and most effective to write affirmations in the present tense. Why, you may ask? Your subconscious mind takes certain things very literally. If you're using an affirmation such as, "I will (lose weight, begin to exercise, etc.)," the subconscious mind may interpret that as, "I'm going to do this someday in the future." The subconscious mind then keeps it as a future goal, not a present goal. In writing and using affirmations, you give your brain a specific direction to move.

Here are a few steps to take when creating affirmations:

1. Find a quiet place where you can think and focus on what you want to achieve.

2. Answer the question, "what do you want?" and make the answer as specific as possible. (For example, "I want to lose 20 pounds," rather than, "I want to lose weight.")

3. Create a mental picture of the change you want. Visualize a thinner version of youself or picture yourself running a 5K.

4. Get a pencil or pen, and write down the goal you are thinking about.

5. Write your affirmation underneath the goal. Make it personal.

6. Start with words such as "I am. . ."

7. If you choose to, include a present tense verb, such as "I show," "I respond," or others.

8. You can also add a positive emotion to the affirmation. "I am excited about..."

9. Finish the affirmation with the results you want. "I am excited about the relaxed person I am becoming."

10. Repeat the affirmation at least twice a day.

Meditation For Confidence

Meditation is a wonderful tool that can be used to master or improve any skill or ability, confidence included. This method often goes unnoticed and is rather thought of in the spiritual sense or as means of stress relief or for calming and relaxing during trying times.

Meditation grants you the power, in that moment to decide the outcome of your own life. The past and the future have no place here and the only thing is now and you. Meditation has the effect of bringing awareness into your mind and if you decide in that moment to boost your confidence, you will.

There are certain tricks you can try to use meditation to boost your confidence and make you feel wonderful about yourself and your abilities. It's time to take charge of your dreams and create your future.

Try to remember what confidence feels like. Think back on past situations where you confidence was at an all time high and try to recall how wonderful it felt to be so in control. Use these positive feelings from past experiences as weapons or tools when approaching new challenges in the present.

Use your meditation to picture future challenges and your success. This is a wonderful way to boost your confidence. Meditation takes practice. The situations you envision should be as detailed as possible. Use those positive feelings from the past where you have felt great confidence and bring them into this situation and envision your success. Focus on the present moment, take what you need from your past experiences and let them go.

We have all had situations where we seem overwhelmed with problems and every thought has negative connotations and very little of the confidence you need to actually overcome the problem or situation. Try very hard to stay in the moment. The past is gone and the future yet to happen but you can control the present moment. Sit quietly, breathing, focus on the moment and you will begin to realize that life is not as complex as it seems to be and this will encourage a calming effect which will allow you to reach for the confidence you need to succeed and overcome these challenges.

There are of course guideline to follow in order to achieve the most from your meditations.

- Find a place where you can be alone with your thoughts, no distractions and no noise.
- Sit upright with good posture
- Breathe, inhale deeply and exhale
- Pause between breathes
- Repeat an affirmation to yourself as you breathe in and out. "I am confident" "I am worthy" "I am capable"

Meditations should be practiced regularly, practice makes perfect as with any skill. As you practice more and more, you will begin to find it easier to close yourself off from the outside world for longer periods. Begin with ten minutes and progress from there.

The more you practice, the easier you will find it to meditate. Your life will be filled with understanding and the confidence you need to succeed and take on any task, no matter how big or small it is. Your inner power will grow in strength and that will propel you to great heights.

It may seem boring at first but persevere through this and incorporate meditation into your daily life. Don't make excuses of why you can't meditate today, ten minutes is all it takes. When you finally do experience that inner confidence and inner peace, it will be well worth it and true happiness awaits.

Affirmations are an important part of meditation and should be part of your daily routine. Some popular affirmations to boost confidence are simple and easy to remember but are extremely effective. They seek to instill belief in you, belief in yourself and in your abilities.

"I live in the present and I am very confident of my future."

"I approve of me, I love myself completely and believe in my abilities."

"I love challenges, they bring out the best in me."

"I thrive on confidence and nothing is impossible. I am capable."

Of course you can think up some of your own affirmations, something that means something to you and is important in your situation. Maintain a positive vibe with your affirmations, no negative emotions are allowed.

Always bear in mind that how others perceive you is heavily reliant on how you perceive yourself. The more confident you are, the more likely to succeed you will become. Believe in yourself, believe in your abilities and realize that you can overcome any challenge in your way. Be grateful for what you have been provided with as gratitude is a positive energy we all should incorporate into our lives. Eat well and stay fit, a healthy mind and body will promote a healthy outlook on life and the challenges it brings with it. Direct your thoughts towards solutions to problems rather than concentrating on the problems. These may all seem like small things but these small things can really impact your confidence in ways you could never imagine.

Feed Your Confidence

Healthy eating is a wonderful way to boost you body image and to improve your confidence. If you love your body and are happy with yourself, you will not have the tendency to shy away from social occasions or to fade into the wallpaper but will have the tenacity to stand up and be heard.

Certain foods are known to boost your confidence. Foods that contain the amino acid called trytophan . This wonder chemical boosts the level of serotonin in your brain. This feel good chemical does just that, makes you feel good. Confidence and over all positive feelings will overcome you and your trials and tribulations will be a thing of the past.

Dark Chocolate contains endorphins which are known to produce feelings of happiness. Phenylethylamine produces serotonin which is that feel good chemical we spoke of earlier. Dark chocolate is known for it's properties which reduce anxiety and stress which in turn will allow you to feel more confident.

Garlic is a wonderful flavoring for food but has it's benefits as well. Eating garlic regularly can reduce the instances of heart disease, reduce your blood pressure and help you lose weight. It has extremely positive effects on brain function and will certainly boost your confidence.

Eat nuts in large quantities. Large quantities of nuts contain serotonin and will have you feeling happier and more content in no time, this positive outlook will lead to confidence.

Eat fruits that will increase the level of serotonin in your body, this will eventually result in a more confident and definitely healthier, you. Kiwis, grapefruits and pineapples trigger serotonin production. If you are feeling weak or depressed, eat bananas, natures gold. The magnesium, potassium and Vitamin B will improve your brain function and a healthy brain is the best way to boost your confidence.

Seafood is known as brain food and is high in serotonin. Eating fatty fish has a wealth of health benefits that all lead to a happier you. Salmon is known to eliminate fat and boost your brain function. A happy and healthy brain will always foster confidence. If you really are not in favor of eating fish, try a fish oil supplement but get your intake daily.

Green, leafy vegetable are amazing sources of serotonin, folic acid and iron. This combination is wonderful for boosting your immune system and triggering the production of serotonin. Your brain function is positively affected. Eat your greens and you will be happier and more confident than ever before.

To be truly confident you have to be happy with your body image, perhaps you are a little heavier than you would like to be and feel a little intimated by those who are slimmer. Take action, this is something you can control. Eat your vegetables and boost your weight loss. A slimmer and more confident version of you is within your grasp. Fill you mealtime menus with spinach, cucumber, carrots, broccoli, asparagus, cabbage, bell peppers, and tomatoes will have you at your goal weight before you know it and you can step out in confidence and take on the world with a winner's attitude.

Exercise for Confidence

You should never underestimate the value of exercise in promoting a general feeling of well-being and boosting your confidence. Without self-confidence, you are more like to take a passive approach to tasks and challenges that life throws your way. You may have a treasure of valuable ideas or information but without the confidence to speak out and act out, nobody is ever going to realize your brilliance. Exercise is a magical tool that can be used to promote a healthier self image and boost your confidence in every way.

Exercising allows you to feel well physically, the healthier you feel physically, the healthier you will feel mentally. Your energy levels are boosted and you feel as if you can take on any challenge and obstacle in your path. Feeling great physically and mentally will foster a positive outlook on life and you will feel strong enough emotionally to pursue life long, personal goals.

A negative self image means that you are not happy with how you look and this leads to a very low self esteem. If you aren't happy with how you look, you won't be happy with the person you are and this negative attitude will seep into every part of your life. How you act, speak, and react will all be results of your negative self image. Someone with such a negative self image will definitely not volunteer their opinions or even wish to stand out from the crowd in any way. Exercising can help to improve your self image. It can result in weight loss and if that isn't forthcoming, toning your body will improve the appearance that you so dislike. You must also remember that exercise encourages the production of serotonin and this chemical is that wonder chemical that really makes you feel good. Seeing changes and developments in your body through exercise will boost your self image and your confidence will follow suit.

Increasing your physical strength has positive effects on your mental strength. Few people realize just how much their bodies can handle and when you finally do, your confidence is increased tenfold. Regular, daily exercise will yield results and some of those results will be noticeable on a daily basis. Physically seeing the positive results will boost your confidence each and every day. It is wonderful moment when you realize that hard work does pay off and you will begin to implement that at every opportunity you can and show off your new found confidence and belief in your own abilities.

Exercising encourages you to set goals and to work towards achieving them. The sense of accomplishment that you receive through meeting small goals is extremely rewarding. Each time you set a goal and you reach it, your sense of confidence will be boosted. You are capable and you will begin to believe in your abilities with each passing milestone.

Exercise is a wonderful way to reduce stress. When you exercise your brain released feel good chemicals that leave you high on life. Relieved of stress, you are able to move through life happier, more relaxed and focused on your goals. Exercise should be done regularly in order to obtain the desired results. Without the weight of stress hanging over you, you are able to face challenges calmly and with clear thoughts and you are better able to manage daily life. In this state, you know that you are in control of your emotions and you are the one who will decide your own fate. Tackling obstacles in this frame of mind will definitely yield results and this will boost your confidence endlessly.

Exercise boosts your brain functioning and cognitive functioning. Exercise is food for your brain and allows your brain access to oxygen and nutrients which it needs in order to function properly. Exercise allows you to feel alert and focused and tasks presented are easily dealt with. Exercise improves your mental function which in turn allows you to complete task efficiently and with ease and this is what ultimately results in the increase in your confidence. Mental and physical wellness enable you with the tools you need to succeed and become the confident person you were born to be.

Exercise is a great way to stay in shape, feed your brain and obtain the level of self confidence that will encourage you to greatness. Feeling great physically and mentally is the perfect way to ensure that you are on top of your game and ready to take on challenges with a clear head, focus, determination and the knowledge that you can do it, even if it seems impossible at times, you can do it and you will.

Confidence Builders That You Can Include In Your Daily Life

Your mind is more powerful than you realize. Your thoughts are what create your emotions, emotions your actions and your actions are ultimately your life. People who display an excellent level of confidence are better in control of their minds and ultimately their lives.

There are things we can learn from people who display great confidence and we can mirror these actions in our own daily lives without much hassle at all if you are willing to apply yourself and are committed to achieving self confidence and a skill that will allow you to make your way to the top of the ladder.

Keep your eye on the prize at all times and don't let anyone or anything distract you from your goal. Formulate a plan to reach your goal and go for it. Don't over think the situation and create unnecessary obstacles.

Confident people maintain a positive outlook. They expect good things to happen to them and as a result they do. Positive vibes breed and attract positive vibes. Expectation is a tool that is powerful and if used consistently and unwaveringly, the results are spectacular.

People who display great confidence act and speak in a way that allows you to believe that they have already achieved their goals when in fact they have not. Their belief in themselves and their abilities is so great that there can be no other outcome.

Confident people know how to use their words and speech. They speak with intent, make their point, what they say is what is going to happen and they are not prepared to accept anything less.

Confident people listen to what others have to say but they do not let what is said affect how they feel, their opinions or the goals. They are not distracted by what others say and frankly don't care either. They have set a goal, created a plan and they will complete it.

Confident people are quite happy to decline offers or requests from others to take on tasks if it is going to affect the energy and time they have for their own priorities. They know what is important and they are going to achieve it.

People who are confident do not brag about their accomplishments. Arrogance and confidence must not be confused. If you are confident in your work then allow your work to speak rather than vocalize it. Your work will say so much more than your words ever could.

Failure is inevitable at some point in everybody's life. You cannot fear failure as it could be the reason that you never reach your full potential. Confident people are confident even in failure as they know this storm will pass and they will once again be on top. Failure is a learning curve and you should take whatever you can from the experience.

Always bear in mind that people are not born confident and those rich and powerful people pasted all over our television screens, were not born that way. They were all once normal people just like you but they believed in themselves and their abilities. Confidence must be practiced daily, the more you practice, the easier it will be to maintain the confident and positive attitude. A lifetime of practice is what it takes, there is no reaching the end in this game, confidence will grow and prosper as long as you keep the attitude and positive mind frame.

WOMEN & CONFIDENCE

Women are often the gender who seem the most stressed or is more easily affected by small obstacles and often lack self esteem and confidence when you compare them with their male counterparts. Women have been proven to respond, behave and act differently in situations where confidence is required. Yes, women are often led to believe that they are the inferior gender but come on ladies, this is not the 1920's and you are just as able, capable and you have just as much ability (sometimes even more) than your male counterparts.

There are things that every woman should know and these factors could impact heavily on their confidence and ability to tackle any obstacle and devise a plan which they will follow through with to ensure their success.

Hormones play a vital role in confidence, how much or how little you have. Men have the upper hand here with their natural production of testosterone. Testosterone is known to reduce cortisol in the body which in turn reduces stress. Men have in some cases almost 100% more testosterone in their bodies than women do so it is easy to understand why they often appear unflappable in situations which often leave women frayed at the edges.

Serotonin, which is the feel good chemical released by the brain, is not as easily processed by women. Serotonin also allows you to feel more confident. Eating sugar is a quick fix when you need that boost of feel good power but long term benefits are felt through regular exercise. Boost those levels ladies and have that feel good feeling pumping you up to take on your next encounter.

Research has shown that women tend to worry and show signs of anxiety about 3-4 times as much as men do and this will definitely lead to lower self confidence levels. The center which control anxiety and worry is twice as big in women as it is in men.

Women often hold back and refrain from taking risks for fear of failure but in cases where they overcome these fears and tackle the tasks and obstacles head on, women perform just as well as men do and as much as men would hate to admit it, sometimes women perform even better.

Confidence is required to take on any task. Our thoughts are converted into actions by our confidence. If your self confidence is high, you will judge your abilities on a higher level than if you lack confidence. Women often underestimate their abilities due to a number of factors and are more likely to take less risks.

Increase in confidence will always result in better performance.

There we have it ladies, you are just as capable and have as amazing abilities as your male counterparts. Don't allow science or social rules to predict who you are, what you have the ability to do and to determine your achievements. Do whatever you can to boost your confidence and get your head in the game. Women are as competent as men, they need only believe in themselves. Women are equal in every way and it's time they realized that and moved out of the corner. Don't wait for your Prince to rescue you, jump on that horse and gallop into the distance on your own and no you don't have to sit side saddle.

Develop Faith

Being positive and having faith in the best outcome is one of the most powerful "processes" that can really change your life big time! And I'm talking in the literal sense. The logic goes this way; when you think about the negative, then negative things will happen. On the other hand, when you think positive, then positive things will also happen to you.

Wake up on the right side of the bed

Being positive is solidly linked to being confident. While being negative is directly related to low self-esteem. For example, when you wake up in the morning feeling already bad about the coming events of your life, then you will really feel down, and your whole day goes like that. You will not feel in the mood and at the same time, your confidence level is also very low.

Try shifting your mood in the positive side. You wake up in the morning and try to empower yourself. Say out loud "I can get through the day with flying colors!" Do this and I can assure you that you will really feel light and driven and this is what fuels you to give your best for that whole day.

But if ever you wake up in the morning and you'll instantly say to yourself that you are a loser and you are a no one, then you will really experience that in reality. You will indeed become a "loser" in things that you will do and this will keep in bringing you down. Take note that at the first place, it's you who have made that kind of decision to be negative and feel like that.

YOU HAVE THE POWER TO INSTILL POSITIVITY

One particular scenario is when you are doing a public speech. A negative man would say to himself words like "you can't do this", "it's too embarrassing", "people will just laugh at you", and other things of the like. He just focused on the negative things and what happens next? He will just confirm his thought that he cannot do it, that it is indeed embarrassing, and people just laughed at him. And again, it's he in the first place that made it happen.

Flipping on the other side of the coin, a positive man would say to himself words like "you can do this", "this is an easy job", "people will like your performance", and other positive things like that. What will happen is that he is able to lift himself up and he has motivated himself to perform well and so it did happen. It's all because that he focused on thinking of the positive and not on the negative ones.

If you are thinking that your feeling is an autopilot and that you can never do anything with it, then think again. You probably grew with a misconception like that. The truth is you have the choice. You have the right to select which point of view you are going to take. And you know for yourself that thinking positive is the only way to make things "positive" and this is the key in making yourself confident. Feel positive and you will feel really confident. As easy as that.

As you continue your quest to become the person that you want to be, don't hold back. But rather reach out and explore what possible potentials you have that is just waiting to be tapped. Be with your own tribe and surround yourself with people that see things like you do. As the saying goes "Once you commit to something, the universe conspires to help you" and that's how you want things to be.

Attract

People have a tendency to be reserved and not show what really interests them. Sometimes it takes a little push to break the ice to start an acquaintance. This can make it difficult to find friends that you want to be with. Rather than waiting, put yourself upfront and get noticed. When like-minded people see what you're up to, you're more likely to be approached by them. As you attract new friends, your tribe begins to grow.

Let Go

Changing your direction in life means having to let go of the things that don't contribute to your objective. Unfortunately, this can include old friends that don't usually support what you're doing. As difficult as it may seem, don't be afraid to let them go. You're most probably be better off without them. For those that agree with you but don't necessarily contribute any help, you can opt to spend less time with them as you get involved with your new tribe.

Be Adventurous

When opening up to a new group of friends, you may find having to do things differently than before. But this does not necessarily mean taking a great amount of risk. Just be open to new experiences broad enough to expand your potentials. So go ahead and grab that back pack and leave the comfort of your home. An adventurous trip with your new group of friends may be just what you need to spread your wings.

Be True To Yourself

Oftentimes, having to fit into a new group of friends can make you feel pressured into doing things that really isn't you. Always remember why you are doing this in the first place. That is to expand your potential and be happy about yourself. So be true to yourself and don't let others make you do things that you're not comfortable doing.

SHOW CONCERN FOR OTHERS

As you are into this for your own gain, remember to also show concern for others. Help your fellow tribe mates also to discover their potentials just as much as you would want them do to you.

WISE MAN SAYS

"It is in the pursuit of happiness where one finds success." And this is what truly matters as you continue your quest to find out what you are made to do. Change is the only constant thing in this world. Some see it from a religious perspective, others see it from a philosophical point of view. No matter how much thought you put into it, we are here for the purpose of others. And this is my share of influence for your journey.

TAKE RISKS

When you stop to take a look inside your mind, you would find so many things like dreams, goals, what ifs, suppressed feelings and the list goes on. Some people treat these things inside their mind as monsters, ones that keep them up at night because of thinking about it and how they are so afraid to battle it.

CHANGE HOW YOU PERCEIVE THEM.

When you look at it closely, looking at all your monsters and considering them as such will hinder you from doing not only one, but all of your goals. All your fears are interconnected that when you want to battle one, you may have to face everything all at once after all just to be able to stand out and make a difference in your confidence.

CHANGE THE WAY YOU LOOK AT RISKS.

These things are not monsters but ones who calls for you to take risks so you can stop being a bud and be a flower in full bloom. What's there to be afraid of risks? They can end in failure yet will reward you with wisdom and confidence or they simply skyrocket you to a better life. Either way, failure or success, both results lead to developing you to be that better version of you. May the risks be small or big, they do affect your overall confidence as it teaches you how to gradually be not so afraid anymore, also no matter how big or small it still makes a difference. So go and take one small risk and start with that, failure or success does not matter, just experience it because it will make you stronger. After you go through one, you'll find that doing another risk the next time won't be as hard. That's confidence from the inside, for you!

The Ways in Which You Can Involve Yourself in Self-Love

Until now you came to know why self-love is important. Now, I'm going to tell you how you'll involve yourself into it and in meantime when you'll be looking at how much you love yourself then there are multiple things which you need to know.

Revolutionary Self-Love, and you.

In a revolutionary world which is so subjective and competitive, and where competition is sometimes so cruel, it becomes compulsory to indulge in self-love. It means love yourself despite everything, what you may have lost and what has been going on, even if you've done something wrong.

Yet, it's sometimes soothing to know that someone else cares for you but love for your own self transcends all. So, it is compulsory for you to love yourself in a committed way by diving into your own soul in the quest for true happiness. The very interesting thing about revolutionary love is that if you have always struggled with your self-respect, it will entirely transform your life.

THE POWER TO RESURRECT YOURSELF:

Whenever you have a powerful sense of loving yourself, it will lead you to taking better care of your health. You will manage your diet in order to nourish your body properly.There are a number of people who manage time for their families and other relations, but they don't make any time for themselves. Please! Don't do this, don't cheat yourself. You need to focus on yourself and your body in order to upgrade your own self esteem, if you don't then you'll lack self-honor which will result in a decline in the habit of loving yourself.

There are multiple ways through which you can start pampering yourself and improve yourself today. Here are some techniques which will help you to upgrade yourself and garner more self worth and affection.

- **Time to relax:** There are many people who take time out to relax in order to give their mind a rest but do so irregularly. So, if you want some fresh perspectives and outcomes then take proper rest of your mind and body.
- **Replace shallow breaths with deep ones:** Sometimes it happens that you take shallow-breaths when you are stressed out and overwhelmed. If you can replace those with some long deep breathes then it will really benefit you. Hold your breath up to your abdomen for 10 seconds then release it for 10 seconds and so on. Repeat this action in order to give some peace and tranquility to your mind and body.
- **Meditate Daily:** Science has proven that stress leads to anxiety and disorder. Meditation is a powerful and useful way to relax your mind, body and spirit throughout which you will be purified from all kind of ambiguities and amalgamations. You may choose your own way to ruminate yourself but do it regularly and properly by fulfilling all the prerequisites. It will definitely benefit you.
- **Do your exercise daily:** A well-known proverb is that a sound body has a sound mind. There is also no doubt that

physical exercise exhausts negative hormones from the human body. So, exercise is particularly crucial for upholding the body and mind equilaterally.

- **Aromatherapy can help you:** This is the ancient art of changing your feelings through multiple and specific kinds of fragrances, flowers, oils and herbs, etc. It has been used for many thousands of years by various cultures all over the world. You can use lavender and chamomile to help yourself rest better at night. If you feel drained of energy, scents like cinnamon, cypress, sage, peppermint, and spiced apple can perk you up. Bergamot, rose, jasmine, frankincense, sandalwood, myrrh, and lemon verdant can ease the pangs of depression and anxiety.

- **Try Showering and bathing:** Relaxing your body via taking bath or shower can be a powerful way to relieve yourself and over indulge in relaxation. You may play music whilst taking a bath to relax the mind. Many people feel comfortable whilst resting in a water tub to revamp their body. You could also shower for a third of the time in hot to warm water, then for about 30 seconds, switch to a colder temperature of water. After this period is up, switch back to the warm water setting for a few minutes. Repeat the process. This switch uniquely provides a light shock to the system that can be comforting and de-stressing. By consistently changing the temperature of the water up and down, you can literally awaken your body and refresh yourself ready to take on the day ahead!

- **Get some fresh air:** Nature is cheaper than any other therapy and is a great place to heal your body and mind. You may notice that by spending time in nature, all your mental fatigue evaporates. Remaining indoors all the time, especially around computers and WIFI is not healthy and does little to improve your self esteem. You can revive your mind by gazing upon nature and just by simply walking outside in nature.

- **Reward yourself:** Its probably common that you are find yourself in a hurry to check on the reaction of others and seek approval. It is important to take reward regardless of what others may think about you. Reward must come from yourself first and foremost, the byproduct of this will eventually be that you will start to notice others do recognise your gifts. The less you care the more you will be noticed anyway!

- **Positive Starts:** The style in which you start your day plays a pivotal role in your life. There must be an optimistic, fresh and healthy initiative by saying goodbye to yesterday's troubles and worries. Be thankful on reopening your eyes after a nights sleep in the morning. Make this a morning ritual and you'll make this a regular habit, it will help harness some positive vibes inside of you to start the day with. Think about any good memories which give you happiness and improve your quality of thoughts. So, by doing this you will be able to transcend the negative feelings which can be the reason of many problems and negative belief systems that we can start the day with.

- **Morning Yoga:** Yoga is a fantastic way of generating energy, strength and improving both the physical body and mind. It's often said by yoga teachers that 'your body can do it, it's your mind you need to convince'! Yoga also helps to stabilize the functioning of the heart, to enhance the flexibility of the body, and will help generate more concentration at work and also to increase a positive outlook on life. By dedicating an hour to yoga on a daily basis it will assist you on the journey to loving yourself more because with the aid of yoga it allows us to use and listen to the inner workings of our mind. Just one month of yoga will help you to feel better and develop deep and long lasting changes within yourself. The byproduct of this will be a much healthier self esteem.

- **Healthy eating:** You should make it a permanent habit to eat healthy food in order to meet all your nutritional needs and to develop a healthy body. A healthy body is a healthy mind and this is vital when developing self esteem. When you start to love and appreciate your body and what you put in it, this will start to radiate outwards and manifest itself as self worth and self confidence. These two really do go hand in hand, therefore, it's of great importance to focus on a good diet to become the best version of you.

- **Journals:** It's very important to write down your thoughts (personal diaries) on daily basis in some kind of journal. It will assist you in reviewing your short comings and weak areas. This useful habit also helps you to highlight your areas of strength. If you don't know how to start this journal then just write from the heart, the more honest and open you are with yourself the better you can identify both areas for improvement and areas of praise. With the help of these journals you will be able to track your progress and areas where you need to focus more on. This will help you to have true picture of where you need to spend more time harvesting self love and self worth. Whilst writing journals you should write down all of your routine jobs and events in detail. I've seen countless amount of people whose habit of writing diaries or journals really does propel them onto the next level . So, the purpose of this helps you to ponder upon yourself which will enable you to love yourself and to see the areas where you might be giving yourself a hard time.

- **Self-help books:** Reading is just like conversation, whereupon books talk but good books listen as well. Good books are like good friends, some times they may give us necessary advise that we may not want to hear which will enable us to grow. We shouldn't just make it a hobby to read books, but we should also try to avoid wasting our time in reading useless books or perhaps glossy airbrushed magazines that fill our minds with trash and make us feel inadequate. Books that empower you and encourage should be essential for developing self esteem. The important point is to apply the lessons that you learn from these books in your everyday life.

- **Good company:** It's an innate habit of human beings that a man or woman acquires many of the behaviours and patterns throughout his environment and the interaction with the people whom he or she spends the most time with. It's therefore said, A man is known by the company he keeps. So, try to adopt good company so that you can inhale positive attitudes from them. You will feel happiness in the company of good people because they direct you towards your real goal, the way to love yourself! People who bring you down or are always critical towards you need to be avoided if you are serious about developing self esteem.

- **Forgive yourself:** We are often very harsh on ourselves when we don't have to be, oftentimes we can become our biggest enemy and our worst critic. Try to overcome this bad habit by trying the following.

  -Move forward by locking past doors so as to not let your past to define you.

  -Don't hold onto the same old conventional stories. Don't follow them blindly, rather keep yourself motivated, move forward and make a new story

  -You must realize that its not just down to others to forgive you, but you also need to forgive yourself, it demands a lot of patience but you can do it!

  -Realize that you tried your best and gave it your best effort at that time. This realization will help you to forgive yourself in certain circumstances. Go easy on yourself and become your own best friend.

- **Be Expressive:** It's also very crucial that you express yourself fully in the world without caring about any outside resistances or criticism. It means to let this world know all about your built-in capabilities or your innate creative gifts. There is nobody else quite like you in this World and you were born with gifts and qualities nobody else has. Don't hold back from embracing these gifts and open your magic box! Most people will live an entire life having not opened theirs, don't let that be you!

- **Seek Happiness:** Happiness doesn't find you but it's you who finds happiness. Here are two questions for you. Is happiness important for you? Are you aware of ways to find it? If not, here are some simple hints to understand the dynamics of how you can seek happiness.

Many times its an option or a choice, you can choose how you're going to start your day. You can attack the day sitively or you can slip into victimhood.

It's all about your mindset. First, train your mind in how to absorb happiness from your surroundings. T

It doesn't depend upon your status in society or your caste. Don't get upset with whatsoever societal rank you have. When you are happy then nothing matters, and you are free from these kinds of mental bondages.

It can be created even when you're going through hard times. We can choose in each moment how we react so you are literally in control! Consider it as a gift and enjoy it by loving yourself!

Self-Introspection: When you develop the habit of an inquiring mind you become aware of yourself. Inspecting your inner mindset and catching yourself in negative thought patterns is an essential tool in developing self esteem. In saying this you shouldn't just ponder your shortcomings but also try to make different parameters of your life. Self-introspection should be a healthy exercise. When you're carrying out this exercise you need to know these steps

- Note down all the problems and also the good points by pondering upon them
- Spend some time noting down your habits and behavioural patterns.

- Believe that there will be better opportunities for you in the future.
- List the areas in which you want to make development in and develop an action plan in how to improve. .
- Make a to-do list of goals from today onwards
- Also think of some suitable alternatives to the more negative responses you might have. How can you reframe these belief systems into something more beneficial?
- Repeat this exercise everydayNow that we know how amazing self-love is, let us try to tackle some sensitive concerns that we might have, i.e. our own shadow. Let's see if you can get through this and leave your baggage behind to embrace your happiness.

Loving yourself may not be that easy for some of us. It is easy to give you all this advice, but doing it is the hardest part. Changing your daily routine and outlook in life takes time and courage. For some it doesn't work at all. Like what the saying says: 'No great things will be achieved without enthusiasm'. Negative thoughts, habits and beliefs should be thrown straight to the garbage can. In this chapter you will learn more about it, and we will help you see that adversity can be overcome.

You need to be the first person to know what your imperfections are, your weakness and limitations; these are the factors which affect our way of thinking, our character and how we love ourselves.

Some of these factors but not limited to are the following:

Appearance generally is how we look physically. This is how we judge ourselves, and that affects your overall personality. You feel good when you look good and bad if you do not like what you see in the mirror. That's why most of us spend a lot of time, effort and money to enhance how we look. Improving how we look is a good and positive approach. However, before we start in self beautification, we should learn to internally see our own beauty from within. No matter how much we improve the way we look, if we choose to look at it differently it will never be enough.

How confident are you with your looks? Do you love your body? Do you think that your colleague or a friend looks better than you? Appreciating is good, but *remember to appreciate yourself as well. Our flaws,* imperfection and impairment does not matter if you appreciate yourself. Your perception in life matters the most.

Social status is how you are being classified in society. This is your rank, achievement and family influence. Various factors can affect one's social status, the likes are: race, ethnicity, skin color, gender, age and religious belief. Social power or dominance is very evident in different group sectors. All of this can contribute to the way you feel about yourself.

Our status confirms the value of our hard work. It is also a good motivator on how we behave in society. Due to its importance it is considered a big chunk in our pie of fully attaining self-love.

Social rejection and oppression can cause us to have a lower capability to enhance ourselves. It will attack your self confidence and self esteem to deal with everyone around you. Knowing how important your status is, is a good beginning in starting your new-found self-love. If you can give that love first to yourself, society is just a factor in this world. Later on we will give some example of how to deal with this struggle.

Relationships with others are important to us. We all know what relationships are and how important they are for us a human being. In society, we seek to be accepted. In a relationship you wanted to be loved and cared for, but you need to be the person that other person needs as well.

A good relationship can give us strength, hope when we seem to be in the dark and love even if we have nothing more to offer. A good relationship with another person motivates us to love ourselves. On the other hand, a bad relationship can ruin our own personality. It will leave a scar and shatter us; a bad relationship will lead you away from who you are, detach you from your life and the things that you love, and sometimes unknowingly away from your dreams.

Relationships with our family, spouse or friends is our basis of who we are right now and who we will be in the future. A strong relationship with others is substantial in seeking happiness, so find that happiness in yourself first, and then you can share it with someone who can give you a moral boost towards happiness.

Perception. Your perceptions of yourself, others, situations, and the life that you live had the power to make or break your sense of self love and confidence. Where one sees a glass ceiling, another may see a boundless sky. One of the trickiest truths about perception is that whatever you are exposed to has the power to change your mind. However, if your perception of life not benefit you, you have the power to alter it until it does.

What you see and understand about life affects what you do. The key factor is always your perception, which is your ability to examine what you are seeing around you and process it in a particular way. Perception is far more critical than you think when it comes to self love and the pursuit of happiness. Two siblings can grow up in the same household and choose *completely different* paths to fulfilment. Two kids can grow up in the same neighborhood and one becomes a doctor or lawyer, while the other pursues a lifetime of crime. Two students can attend the same college and be exposed to the same temptations, while one graduates and another flunks out. Two people can read the same book, and one may forget about it, while another takes action and revolutionizes their life with the information. What do you perceive?

Life experiences. Whilst life gives us a lot of learning and achievements, we cannot disregard the fact that it also leaves us with pain and scars. Good experiences can be a source of self confidence and help us find more meaning to life. It can aid us in overcoming obstacles and pressure in life.

According to some psychologists, remembering negative memories is human nature. Quite true right? Our negative experiences carve in our head that a single word can trigger it every day. Our own character is made of it, and for some who have experienced drastic and unimaginable experiences, they choose it to define themselves; from the way they look physically, how they interact with other people and how they see themselves. Sometimes those negative experiences are all they have to survive.

Not all are the same in accepting negative experiences and positive experiences. There are a few who cannot determine the difference. The person who has self-love can overcome this struggle and will be able to find happiness, not because he/she had experiences but simply because he/she chooses to be happy.

These statements are examples of how negative perception can affect you, and how you can overcome it.

"How can I love my fat body? I hate it!"

This struggle is top of the list. Obesity and being overweight is a condition where the body gains excessive fat and you are not alone in this battle. Most people, fat, thin, or in-between, have issues with their bodies. When you look at yourself in the mirror and you hate what you see, you are ashamed of yourself. It's either you're too fat or too thin. You're legs are short or you don't have curves, etc.

We cannot change our physical appearance overnight, by meditating, or by prayer; it needs work and yes, it is a long run. If you want to be happy, you need to drop those self pitying and negative beliefs in your head. A person who loves him/herself accepts his/her imperfections and knows his/her strengths. We can start by altering our perspective.

There are some great tips in the next chapter which will surely help you. For now, here are some tips to overcome and help you show your inner beauty.

1. **I am beautiful! - Mantra**. Don't just say it. Believe in it, because it is true. Try looking at yourself every morning naked in the mirror and recite that mantra. If you have doubts in believing in it then find good things about yourself, and say it aloud! "I am a beautiful creature with hands to use and legs to take me to places today!" "Another beautiful day to use my awesome brain. Oh, I'm so smart and lovable." It may be unstylish but who cares. If it's about you, it is worth it. Have the courage to embrace yourself and what you are made of.

2. **Dress code.** Yes, we have to adhere, but this is not to stop you from wearing what is in trend today, this is to make you feel comfortable about yourself. You do not want to ruin your day just because you can't fit in a dress or pair of pants you just bought. Buy clothes that fit you and underwear too. Dress in your own style and size.

3. **Health is wealth.** When you choose to have your lunch in Taco Bell or Burger King today think about yourself first. What your body needs isn't what your appetite desires. Those fast-foods are very convenient indeed, that's why they are successful! When you eat something, think about yourself, of what is truly good for you.

4. **Move.** As we know how important exercising is, let me just emphasize that this is not you burning fat to be sexier (though that would be great, wouldn't it?). Exercise at least 30 minutes a day, believe me your body needs it more that you know. All you might be seeing is your imperfections, and you think that exercising is a long process that you'd rather not do, because it won't work, or at least you think it won't. In case you forgot, you're a human being and aside from your external parts, you have internal organs that needs attention as well. If you can't bring yourself to join the gym, start with walking. Make sure you do it every day for an hour.

Our physical appearance is the first thing we notice about ourselves. Learn to accept and love yourself first. Walk in the street feeling lucky that you are alive. Do not lose that confidence when someone looks at you or throws some nasty glance at your imperfections. Everyone has one. It is the ones who love themselves most who will win the day, and sleep well at night.

Arguments Against Self Love. Many individuals face blocks to self love by the experiences that they had in life, or the negative opinions of others that were ingrained in them as a child. As a result, these individuals tell themselves that they are unworthy of self love on some level. Many of these arguments are a result of the words and ideas that you choose to accept. If you are not careful, these arguments against self love can become excuses and destructive beliefs that can hold you back from progress in life and inner peace within your heart, soul, and mind. When the person who makes you feel bad is it was someone important to you, the blows to your self esteem are very real. Although you may have allowed these negative encounters and memories to bother you, you can make the decision to not let it destroy any more of your life and self worth. You can learn to love yourself again, and you can do so unconditionally.

"I was abused as a child and was told, I deserved it. "

Most victims of childhood abuse fail to attain self-love. Some psychologists reviewed that most of them think or believe that they deserve it. It is not surprising because when the act of abuse is current, you were probably yelled at that you are a bad kid or what you did is wrong or you were told not to do it - that you deserved it. In a child's understanding they believe it, because they love the abuser; it could be their parents or guardian, and as a child all we want is to please these people to gain their love and attention. We also believe that they are hurting us because they love us.

Let's get a thing straightened out first. What is abuse? A corrupt practice or custom: unjustly. By the meaning of the word itself it should figured. Being abused is never your fault. The abuser may have found happiness or contentment in abusing. It may be physical or verbal. Abuse is abuse. It is their problem not yours to deal with. You do not deserve to be a punching bag, you do not deserve to take all those condemning words because they are angry or impatient. It wasn't out of love or affection. It was not done to discipline you.

An abuser may be your parents, sibling or guardian. You are expecting love and caring from them so you think it is the right thing to do, that they have the right to inflict harm on you. Sadly, those people were not thinking about your welfare when they were doing the act of abuse. If these people really care and love you they could never do those things. No matter what reason they have, or reasons they want you to believe that you deserve it, it's just not true, because before they do anything they have a choice, a choice to hurt you or love you - they choose to harm you. That is not love, that is not caring. As a victim you also do not have a choice to change your past or *start a new life*. You only have one so you cannot change it. You may not change your past but you can always work on your ending.

Why not try new things? If it's too hard for you go out, then start with yourself.

1. Read books that talk about how a person overcame life after being abused. 11 Minutes of Paolo Coelho is about a prostitute and how she retained her self-esteem and end up confident about her future.

2. Attend meeting with people who have had the same experiences. Do not be ashamed of your experience, be proud that you been through a real rough experience and be thankful that you are alive.

3. Find your dreams. Your life doesn't end after the stormy night. Even if you want it to or not, the sun will always shine - look forward to it and own your future. Be brave and follow your dreams.

You might be asking 'how can I start? Do I have what it takes to be happy?' You can answer that question by yourself. Start loving yourself and appreciating life. You might think life is unfair for you. It is true. Life is unfair. Because life doesn't care what you think or what will happen to you. It is you who will be responsible for it. Stop telling yourself that you deserve being abused. You will only deserve it if you think you do and continue agonizing yourself for the rest of your life. Be thankful. Always. This is the key to moving on.

"I do so much to please others and they do nothing in return."

This statement is proof of low self-esteem and a lack of self-love. It is true that we need to get others' approval and acceptance to boost our own confidence, that having someone trusting you can be a good motivator to do better. However, before we move to that step we need to ready our self first.

Do not expect anything from anyone. They do not owe you anything. We might have given them the moon and stars from the sky but you cannot expect them to give you the sun. You give because you are capable. You have something to offer to them and they accepted it. By giving you do not expect anything in return. Learn to be compassionate. Be grateful that you were able to provide and help.

Here are some tips to divert your attention in pleasing others:

Sports. If you're into one, good. If not, then this the time to start. Just a simple sport that you can do like tennis or even chess, it doesn't have to be a professional thing, it doesn't have to be huge, just something you like and enjoy. In sports you need to win but you do not need to please your opponent. Most athletes have a good sportsmanship. If you play good and fair you gain their respect. It is also a good diversion and reason for you to be social.

Socialize. Not social media. Go out and meet new people from different parts of the world or different professions. Get involved in a charity event or social environment, or group travel. All that stuff is there, just look and you will see. A wide world awaits you, and it's fun to meet new people because they will be interested in you, and you in them.

Travel. We mentioned this before, but traveling is one best therapies for a weary heart. Get out and go to places you have never been to. If you have time and a budget go out of town, perhaps go to the beach. Look in every place you visit, observe the people there, and see that everyone is living. People do not care where you're from or what you do. They are living, and so are you. Look into that ocean and see how huge it is and how small you. It is essential for you to develop self-love in order to live your life happily. With the procedures presented in this book , a person who had this experience can overcome the negativity he or she had experienced before. This can be a realization for you to find a new path and start building a good relationship with yourself. Later on, you can be the exact opposite of what others said you are supposed to be. Did they call you a loser? Say that you were a Nobody?_ You_don't have to be a loser, and you are somebody important!_Those are just words and will remain as it is until proven true. And your perception of the truth and circumstances are mutable, and can change at any given time.

Even if it is any truth to the words that were said, you must always remember that you have the power to change yourself. Don't make the mistake of being "stuck in time" with words of the past. What was true 5,10, or 20 years ago does not have to be the truth of the moment. What was said in the past does not have to be resurrected in your life today.

When a person lacks self love, it can feel like what was said way back then is still true today. A young man who was criticized as a child for being out of shape may still feel like a chubby kid inside, even though he has the frame of a model or bodybuilder now. The girl who felt like an ugly duckling as a kid may still see her former self even as others pass by her and gawk at her supermodel features or stunning shape. The Ivy League IT graduate with a job making more than $100,000 a year may still feel like he is not smart enough in some way because of what a negative parent said, over and over again. A man who grew up thinking that he would never be successful may presently have a good, stable job, owns his own home, and is raising a healthy family may still feel like he is not a success because of the harsh words spoken by his father or mother many years before.

To start getting on you can try this things:

Walk. Walking is good habit not just for your body but also for your mind to think. Assess yourself. Ask yourself a lot of questions. Do not be afraid. Think deeper and find out what it is that you really want to do. Find your strength. Do not stop until you have answers to your question. Do this for an hour a day.

Do one different thing in a day. Doing something new can help you discover things about yourself as well, like watching a movie alone, asking your childhood friend out for a movie, visiting a haunted house - anything that is possible and legal.

Follow your dreams. Do what you want, do what you're good at, and indulge in your passions.

Pain is good, and quite healthy as well. It confirms that you are alive and normal. How to go through with it? Self-love. Be thankful of what you have. The more you are thankful, the more you will appreciate life. The more appreciations you give in your life, the better you feel every day. Let go of the things that you cannot change and the things that you cannot have. That doesn't mean your value is less, it just means it is not good for you.

OVERCOMING STRUGGLES

In the previous chapters we tackled the struggle of attaining self-love and how we can deal with it in order to achieve more of it in our lives.

ACCEPT YOURSELF AND BE COMPASSIONATE.

In our daily lives, we never have the control over the things around of us. For example, we cannot change the behaviors and approaches of other people towards us. We cannot change our physical appearance i.e., skin/eyes color, hair style, natural body language etc. The only thing in which we can control is our own perception of ourselves. Take all of the unpleasant events or rude behaviors you have received from the other people with a pinch of salt. This doesn't mean blind acceptance, boundaries are important, but accepting that you cannot change people or past events can go a long way towards healing.

BE THANKFUL

After passing through your choppy past, finally you're in the present moment now. So, be thankful that you have been shown the lessons you needed to learn and if you do the necessary work on yourself then hopefully you will be rewarded for facing your own personal 'dark knight of the soul'.

Be positive and keep in mind that the whole of the day, and indeed the rest of your life, is ahead and that your best years are yet to come! Be determined and don't sweat the small stuff. Sometimes our worst nightmares can actually, in hindsight, become our greatest gifts. If you can change the way you view things then the things you view can change.

Remember also everyone is fighting their own battles in life. Again thats not to say that you should put up with whatever they throw at you, but having that awareness that many of us are also struggling can sometimes make it easier to understand why some people behave the way they do.

- **Dealing with depression** Depression is the enemy of self-esteem. It is a factor which devastates your comfort zone even if good things are happening to you. So, try to become aware when depression sets in because this element will tear up your self-confidence as you start to talk negatively about yourself.

Identify the source of the depression. This act may be one of the best things that you can do to develop a higher level of self-love. Because some people don't bother to undergo this process which results in the lack of healing your wounds.

Bad things may happen to everyone in normal life. So watch your thoughts and if you feel yourself slipping away into a sea of negativity shift your energy, maybe a walk in nature or a yoga class. Its easy to slip into a depression if you lack self esteem, being aware of this fact is the first part of protecting yourself. Be brave and do what you need to do to overcome these hurdles.

- Resolve relationships or set healthy boundaries.

Sometimes we have tough decisions to make. People who we love, close friends or work colleagues can constantly test our patience to the limits. Many people in this World are damaged and feel the need to damage others. Knowing whether to forgive or set healthy boundaries is key. There is a general misconception that just because someone is family or a blood relative that we constantly have to go back to the empty bowl like a dog. You have the right to walk away from ANYONE in your life who oversteps the mark.

Oftentimes we will stay for months or years longer than we should in unhealthy and toxic relationships which only end up damaging us more in the long run.

Sometimes we get so used to being treated like dirt that it becomes a vicious cycle that we seemingly cannot escape.

The good news is that you CAN escapc, and on the path of developing self esteem, hanging around energy vampires is not going to get you where you need to go!

There is nothing wrong with forgiveness, but only when you feel ready. Has the person apologised? Do they feel remorse? Healthy boundaries are critical on the path of self love. It can feel scary at first but you'll eventually be glad you put them in and will probably wonder why you hadn't done it earlier in the end!

On the contrary, if you do decide to forgive a person do so wholeheartedly. There is no point in bringing up dirt from the past time and again if you already decided to forgive and move on.

As always balance is key, healthy boundaries is right up there when you're talking about a healthy self esteem.

LAWS OF SELF-LOVE

HOW DO I LOVE MYSELF?

We must ask this question to ourselves. We used to fall in love often, forgive the people of their mistakes but why don't we forgive ourselves of our own mistakes?

It's different to indulge in self-love because sometimes you fail to accept yourself in your purest form and might start searching for the ways to escape. Some of you may even try to to run from yourselves. Why do we do this? Do we feel we don't deserve love subconsciously? If this is the case then more self inquiry is needed and perhaps a large dose of inner child work to get to those subconscious wounds that maybe holding us back.

If you're looking to do some inner child work or subconscious intervention I would highly recommend the work of Anastasia Moroney at Emotional Sovereignty her website is

www.emotionalsovereignty.com

info@emotionalsovereignty.com

She is one of the best at what she does and has helped me immensely on my own healing journey.

Understand the laws of self-love on your journey. Here are some progressive steps which will help enhance the love that you have for yourself.

THINK SELF-LOVE.

It's a well-known fact that we can change everything with the power of thinking because it's our thoughts which become our belief systems.

To achieve positive thoughts, you may practice meditation, you may start by writing journals etc. This world has both good and bad people. There is always some good in bad and some bad in good. So, try to focus on positive aspects to move forward and to stay on the path of self-love.

DO SELF-LOVE

Try to find happiness in having less by bridging a minimalistic approach of life. Because sometimes having less could prove to be more at times.Start taking care of your body by taking in proper nutrition and a healthy diet to gain good health.

Do proper exercise in order to maintain physical fitness. Practice meditation to purify your mind from all kinds of negative beliefs you may have about yourself.

Commitment and daily practices will get you to where you need to go. It may not be a quick fix but if you can implement good habits daily then you will make huge strides in no time.

ABSORB SELF-LOVE

Look at the beauty in life, the birds, a song you like, or just going for a simple walk. Take time to allow the good stuff to soak into your mind. Focus on the things you take for granted I guarantee it will shift your perspective.

Instead of buying materialistic things, surround yourself with things that don't have an expiry date. For an instance, you may learn a new language, learn how to sing, or you may seek to play a musical instrument.Develop your passion and evolve yourself with the passage of time finding new hobbies and joys which will make you feel good about yourself.

As I have said previously try to surround yourself with positive people. People who are encouraging, interested and that are going to lift you up. Connect with successful people and uplifters because the byproduct will be that you yourself will become more uplifting.

RETAIN SELF-LOVE

As you start absorbing self-love there may come a point when you may start to trigger others with your new found attitude to yourself and life itself. People may try to bring you down or they simply won't like the changes they see in you. Others may start to become jealous of your new found confidence.

Don't let this affect you and keep pushing on, as I have said before there are energy vampires out there so don't give into their toxic ways, keep striving forward.

EXIST IN SELF-LOVE

In a radical world of uncertainty, don't look outside of your own self to preserve self-love because its deficiency will trick you. All the great things come from within, its an incredible insight to know that what we seek from the outside we have to seek within ourself first and foremost. Don't jump into the ocean of ambiguity rather try to exist in the state of self-love. This act will surround you with a concrete sphere around yourself in order to keep you separate from all negative streams.

FEED SELF-LOVE

It may sound awkward when I say feed self-love. It's a journey, not a destination. Up until now, you may succeed in attaining and existing in self-love. Now it is up to you to take the baton and run with it. Keep on watering the flower of your own soul by taking care of the strategies outlined in this book. Spin those plates and take care of your inner World, physical body and spiritual path. As Buddha said 'no one in this entire universe deserves our love more than ourselves' and not a Truer word has been spoken.

These five laws will assist you to achieve the finest form of self-love.

The Importance of Achieving Your Dreams

The art of achieving self-love lies in making yourself happy. Have you set any dreams or goals in childhood or anytime in the past? Have you ever dreamed about becoming a pilot, a doctor, a nurse, an engineer, a footballer, writing a book or travelling to Thailand? Well, if you want to love yourself, then you need to focus on you and your dreams. All of those dreams that you disregarded or you labelled them, 'Forgotten' or 'Unachievable'

Nothing in this world is impossible it just depends upon how badly you wish for it. If you want something, you'll work hard for it and the chances are you can achieve it. When you want something; all the universe conspires in helping you to achieve it you just have to put the work in.

When we achieve our goals it gives us a sense of achievement and that is a great tool in developing self esteem. It means we understand that we don't have to necessarily rely on others and it opens the floodgates to what is truly possible.

- **Seek Success without defining yourself by failure**

Some people find it difficult to indulge in self-love because they define themselves by failures rather than their successes.There isn't any substitute for self-love. There are some people who work a lot and become successful in achieving plenty of success but they still fail when it comes to self-love. These kinds of people are known as overachievers or workaholics. A workaholic is a person who works compulsively. While the term generally implies that the person enjoys their work, it can also alternately imply that they simply feel compelled to do it. These kinds of people often surround themselves with a heavy work load in order to disguise their true feelings that they may have about themselves and their lives. So its important that we don't use success to mask our inner World in such a way that it becomes just another firefighter for our subconscious wounds.The sad thing about it is that there is just a masking process going on, they have developed in one area of life but forgotten the most important.

There is an excess of such people who earn far less than overachievers and workaholics, but they look happier because they fall in love with themselves. Unfortunately, it's just due to a negative philosophy of western society. I have travelled extensively and some of the poorest people I have come across often look the happiest.

People who love themselves always emit rays of positivity while people who lack self-love almost always see the negative aspect of life.One of the biggest differences between optimistic people and pessimist people is what they decide to focus on. So, always choose to see the positive perspectives of your life when possible.

How your achievements help you to attain complete self-love

To ponder upon this statement, you may ask two questions

Is it a quick process?

Is it a long journey?Always be realistic about the time frame of your journey. How much time will it take you reach your destination? While doing this, keep one thing in mind, don't rush because if you do then you may fail and get demotivated which will dishearten you. During the process of your journey, the supplements of self-love will feed you to remain inspired. Small victories over time will build your self confidence as you go.

- **Re-evaluate in the midpoint of the process**

At the midway of your journey pause your efforts for a while. Reconsider your goal and reevaluate yourself, do you still want it?. If you are still self-determined, then proceed forward.

- **The gift of clarity** This point demands a lot of thought because it's very important to clarify your dreams moving forward. So, take as much time you need to to clarify your goals as it's so important to elucidate your vision. So, don't hesitate to design your goals that really reflect your inner desire.

As Stephen Kellogg says that 'It's better to be at the bottom of the ladder you want to climb than at the top of the on you don't'.

- **Using S.M.A.R.T goal setting**

Set your goals according to your own level because if you fail in achieving your goals then you may feel disheartened which might start negative mind loops about yourself. Setting and achieving a series of small goals is one strategy to overcome this factor. It will be far better having small victories than to become desperate midway. Baby steps to get to your destination can often prove much more beneficial than massive strides where things may get missed or rushed.

So, try to utilize the S.M.A.R.T terminology to achieve your goals. What does the SMART acronym mean?

S SpecificM Measurable

A Attainable

R Relevant

T Timely

- **Specific**

Your goal shouldn't be vague or unclear. It shouldn't be too general, rather it should be so clear and specific that you can easily plan a map for your journey.

- **Measurable**

Whenever you decide to plan your goals, then make predetermined steps. Set ways to measure your progress. In this way, you'll be able to check your progress in the future. It will also enable you to resume your journey if you get stuck at any point.

- **Attainable**

Use cognition reasoning to design goals while finalizing your ambitions. Consider all of the realities and outward stimuluses i.e temperature, environment etc. and all available resources i.e., labor, time etc. It's will help you to determine whether or not if this goal is attainable.

- **Relevant**

This is a very basic step in the process. In setting your goals ponder upon these questions first.

- What are the reasons to opt for this goal?
- Does it match with your lifestyle/interests/personality?
- Feasibility given your capabilities?
- Why you're choosing this goal, either you're selecting it for yourself or for someone else?

- **Timely**

Timing is key to accomplishing your goals. Set a time frame to attain. It must not be too short, nor too lengthy, rather fitting according to the measurements worked out previously.

By using the techniques of SMART, we may concisely prepare ourselves to attain our goals using a solid strategy which minimises failure or disappointment and can help build our self esteem.

As Michelangelo says 'the greatest danger for most of us isn't that the aim is too high and we miss it, but that it's too low and we reach it'

- **You must preserve**

Scott Reed says that this one step-choosing a goal and sticking to it changes everything.

Sometimes, people have similar ideas and strengths but their will power to persevere is the main factor that separates the two. Many times, the winner of the race or achiever of solid success aren't the smartest people but the ones who strived hard to achieve whilst taking care of obstacles that came their way.

- **On goal accomplishment**

Achieving a goal or dream, is a fast track to self-love. One of the best ways to boost your self-worth is to figure out one of your dreams, or make a list of goals, and start accomplishing them. The more you achieve your dreams the more self confidence, self love and self esteem you will build.

Upon reaching your destination, you may ask these questions

Did you feel bliss when you achieved a goal?

Did you feel proud of yourself?Did attaining your goals, arise a sense of accomplishment ?

Did you improve your life or the lives others?

- **Importance of rewarding yourself**

Don't wait for others to reward you, rather reward yourself when you accomplish a goal. It doesn't matter how small it is just do yourself a favor and give yourself a reward. Reward yourself by celebrating it. Don't ever forget to acknowledge yourself and your achievements before switching to next goal.

It will invigorate you, drive you forward and is the ultimate self esteem booster!

The advantage of setting solid goals cannot be ignored if you want to achieve success and accomplish things that benefit you, your loved ones, or even society. Fortunately, you can follow a tried and proven system to expedite your plans for success."

Facts About Confident People

Confident people may come off as cool, calm and collected in the face of stressful situations but they are human, just like you are, they just know how to mask their emotions in order to maintain their composure.

Confident people, although they may appear calm and collected, also suffer from anxiety, and nervousness and also experience that awkward feeling we all dread. They are human and they do feel those nervous flutters, they have just mastered the art of keeping it inwardly focused. It doesn't matter how confident you are, nervousness in front of a crowd is normal and that feeling never goes away. Learn to deal with it as you become more confident and keep that cool and calm exterior.

Confident people are more easily able to manage their emotions. Yes, the feel the emotions they have just learned how to control what is shown on the outside, only allowing emotions that are appropriate for that moment, escape. Managing your emotions takes time and practice and you have to learn to set the right mindset to deal with the situation. Your emotions should not be allowed to guide your actions. You have the power to control the situation.

People who display a huge confidence are often those who have performed or spoken in front of large audiences for a very long time. They admit to feeling the nerves beforehand but once on stage their natural instinct to perform takes over. Their skills have been acquired through routine and repetitiveness.

Confident people are not afraid to let people see their weaknesses or their vulnerability. They take risks even when failure is a possibility. They don't allow failure to define who they are. They are open and willing to take criticism and learn and grow from it but at the same time, they don't define themselves by what others think of them. They know their own worth and that is why they have that wonderful feeling of confidence and security. Know your own worth and your life will be full of pleasure and the failures won't be as hard to handle.

That actor who seems so calm in any role or the teacher who seems so at ease speaking to halls full of students, they feel the same fears as you do, they simply know how to manage that fear and the emotions that go along with it and present an exterior that is calm and confident. Lessons that are learned through time and practice. Take your time, nothing worth possessing is easy to obtain or hold on to. Persevere and you will reap the benefits of your hard work sooner than you may think.

CONCLUSION

Your fate lies in your own hands. It is up to you to take control of your life, your emotions and situations presented to you and negotiate your way safely to the other side.

There is no time to hold back or to be afraid of taking that risk in case you fail. Failure is going to happen whether you like it or not but that shouldn't be something that you allow to define you or whether you decide to take risks in the future. Failure teaches you, learn what your failures have to offer, process the information and realize how you could have done it differently and you are assured that next time you will achieve the success you are after.

Everybody is built unique and with their own personal quirks and flaws. Learn to love yourself for who you are and realize how much you have to offer to the world. Your abilities are there, you just need to take the time to seek them out without allowing all the negative or weak point get in the way. As humans we have a tendency to place too much emphasis on the negative and not enough of the positive. Don't allow your weaknesses to overshadow your brilliance hidden within. What a sad and boring world it would be if everybody was built the same, with the same abilities and capabilities and perfect in every way. We all have something to offer and that is what makes the human race such a diverse and interesting species. The trick through all of this is to learn to appreciate yourself and acknowledge your strengths and make a concerted effort to improve those abilities.

If you are someone who has a low self image, don't sit back, take control and do something today that you will thank yourself for in the future. You are the one who controls how you feel about yourself and you are the one who can change what you are not happy about. Realize what it is and do something to rectify that situation. The sooner you do, the sooner you will bloom into the wonderful, charismatic, confident individual you were put on this Earth to be.

You are your own person in every way. Don't ever allow others to make you feel less than adequate, stand your ground and let them know that you are amazing and you deserve to be treated as such. What others think of you is not your problem, it is their problem. Do what makes you happy, believe in something with conviction and stand up for it, make decisions and don't quit even in the face of failure and always walk with you head held high. You were not created to blend into the wallpaper, you were given a voice so use it wisely and let people know your opinions even if you may seem silly after the fact.

Eat a healthy diet and follow an exercise regime. Your mind and body need the stress release. The oxygen and nutrients will provide you with enough energy and strength and of course stamina to take on whatever life throws your way. A healthy body and mind allows you to focus on what is important to aim for those goals.

Don't compare yourself to others. You are an individual and you need to realize that. Yes, watch how other more confident people approach certain situations and learn from them. Take criticisms but don't take them to heart. Process them, take what you need from them an move on.

Never compromise what you feel or believe for the sake of fitting in. We were not made to fit in but rather to stand out and you should.

Confidence is something that starts within yourself. You need to be happy and content with yourself and realize your own potential before you can expect anybody else to. Take charge and make changes, be happy with you first and the confidence will follow. Carry positive thoughts with you and visualize good things for you and you will find that they will find you, don't expect anything less that what you want. Expectation is a very powerful force which you should use to your advantage.

Yes, of course there will be days where you feel like you are coming apart at the seams but these are just life's little challenges presented to you along the way to success. Stay positive inside and out. Even on days when you feel blue, put on your confident strut and hold your head high, you will find that your mind will follow suit .Your mind does whatever you will it to and if you steer it in the right direction you will know what it feels like to truly live.

Confidence will allow you the opportunity to meet new people, strike up conversations with complete strangers and you never know what the future holds. We often get stuck in a rut within our own personal relationships and block our partners out. Let them in and reveal a side of you they have never seen and get that spark ignited. Flirt a little, be friendly and welcome new people into your life. Yes, they may not be there for long but they may end up being there for a lifetime.

Take every opportunity that comes your way and grab it with both hands, even if you fail at least you won't have regrets about what might have been. Be confident in your decisions and if they don't work out for you so be it but do it again anyway. Don't delay your progress by waiting for the perfect moment, we all know the moment will never be perfect and there will always be some kind of obstacle. The sooner you realize that you are only using this tactic out of fear of the unknown and fear of failing, the better. Embrace your fears and take the leap and you will be amazed at how exhilarated you feel.

I do hope this book has inspired those who are lacking in self esteem and confidence to realize that they are in control and that the sooner they become happy with themselves and believe they are capable of great things, the sooner their lives will truly begin. Nobody is inferior to anyone else, some people have just realized where their strengths lie and have taken full advantage but it's not too late for those who have yet to realize so stop thinking " what if" and "if only" and close your eyes and jump. Allow the world to see you brilliance in all it's glory. We all posses that brilliance just in different ways and what you may think is insignificant could be a talent that many can only dream of possessing.

You are your keeper and your master and you control your body, your mind and your emotions. You are the one who determines your future and how the world perceives you. Stand up and take a bow, the world is waiting.

I do hope that this book has been a helpful start on your journey towards more self love. If you have enjoyed my work please consider leaving a review on Amazon as it really does help both my work and spreading these important messages and techniques.

You may also want to consider my other book which dovetails this topic called 'The Codependency Recovery Roadmap-Empowering Strategies And Steps For Successful Codependency Rescue' Thank you in advance.